Archibald Lampman

VOLUMES READY IN THE RYERSON SERIES

Critical Views on Canadian Writers

MICHAEL GNAROWSKI, *Series Editor*

CRITICAL VIEWS ON CANADIAN WRITERS

Archibald Lampman

Edited and with an Introduction by
MICHAEL GNAROWSKI, Series Editor

THE RYERSON PRESS
TORONTO WINNIPEG VANCOUVER

ISBN 0-7700-0297-8

Every reasonable care has been taken to
trace ownership of copyrighted material used
in this book. The author and the publisher
will welcome information that will enable
them to rectify any errors or omissions.

PRINTED AND BOUND IN CANADA
BY THE RYERSON PRESS

To
NEIL COMPTON

ACKNOWLEDGMENTS

I am indebted to Joy Andison, Louise Carpentier and Angela Lindy of the Library, Sir George Williams University, for their unfailing kindness and friendly interest; and to Ilene Rapoport for help with the manuscript, and other valuable assistance.

M.G.

CONTENTS

Archibald Lampman

INTRODUCTION

Archibald Lampman's published career may be said to cover a period of eleven years, in the course of which time he saw the publication of two collections of his poetry and was guiding his third volume into its final stages at the time of his death. If we can accept then that there were three Lampman collections between 1888 and 1899, we must also note that two of these were privately published and that only *Lyrics of Earth* had found an outside publisher in Copeland & Day. As a matter of fact, as poet and literary personage, Lampman did not impress as the most considerable figure of that late nineteenth century phase in Canadian poetry. Of the four major poets of the Confederation Group, it was Lampman who was most retiring in his literary performance and most tragically fated in his personal life. This is to say that Lampman never enjoyed that professional success as a writer which came to Carman and Roberts, nor did he have anything like the steadily satisfying career of Scott. Yet, even a casual look at a check list of Lampman criticism will show that the poet's work received serious attention in his lifetime and steady appraisal over the last three quarters of a century. Lampman, therefore, had secured critical acceptance for his work from the early beginnings of his mature cycle.

There is no real need, in this instance, for another account of Lampman's life. In this respect he has been well served by the early studies of Connor and Guthrie and, in more recent times, by Desmond Pacey and Munro Beattie. The biographical side of the poet—and there is a good deal of biography in the critical selections which follow— stands fairly well revealed, although there is an unfortunate diffidence in Arthur Bourinot's editing of some of the Lampman correspondence. But it is Lampman's critics and reviewers who concern us here, and I would like to turn to them.

The critical response to *Among the Millet* (1888) was more than respectable, and the book and its author were favourably noticed by no less a figure than William Dean Howells. In a thumbnail review, Howells quoted Lampman's sonnet "The Truth," substantial portions of the five sonnet sequence "The Frogs," as well as the entire poem "Heat," italicising those lines which, he said, ". . . seem to us blest with uncommon fortune of touch where all is excellently good." He concluded by saying:

It is no part of our business to guess
his future; but if he shall do no more
than he has already done, we believe
that his fame can only await the knowledge
of work very uncommon in any time.

(*Harper's,* LXXVIII, 1889, 823)

Curiously, and perhaps significantly, Howells not only advanced a modest claim to having discovered Lampman but established, as well, certain approaches to the poet. Howells characterized Lampman as a poet of Nature; as a descriptive poet; and as a particularly able writer of sonnets. Criticism which would come later would tend to revolve around these elements to the detriment of a full exploration of Lampman's performance as a lively mind and articulate thinker with a range which has not been fully tested to this day. These qualities were hinted at in the Duncan Campbell Scott Memoir, and in Scott's letter to Ralph Gustafson which is reproduced in the latter part of this collection. Additional evidence exists in the Lampman papers in the Public Archives.

Early Lampman criticism tended to stress the poet's connection with Nature, and to develop his reputation on the basis of his descriptive powers and his preoccupation with the natural scene. The first paper in this collection is a good example of the earlier approach to Lampman, and it has the additional value of giving us some idea of Lampman's stature as an established name in contemporary American periodicals. But this immediate if narrow approach had to be expanded, so that in the essay by Barry we encounter what could be described as a full-dress treatment of Lampman. Here, the biographical element emerges as a major concern of critics, and the discussion revolves around Lampman's role as a national poet coupled with his interest in Nature and the general "descriptiveness" of his work. Barry recognizes Lampman's particular skill with the sonnet, and makes one further point. This has to do with what is described as the absence of the human element from Lampman's poetry. The Barry paper, then, is built around recognized and well established elements of Lampman criticism, and it is interesting to see how successive critics, working with given materials, add to the structure.

The Stringer paper, although brief, has a certain originality about it. First of all, it recognizes the well-known features and the standard qualities of Lampman. He impresses as a nature poet, and his role is perceived as that of a *truly* Canadian and, therefore, of a national poet. But Stringer also raises points which will become significant issues for later critics. He attacks "boosterism" (he calls it "booming") and he cautions against the uncritical "booming" of a literature and its writers as a way of making up for inadequacy of performance. Far more interesting though, is the problem of so-called morbidity in young poets (among these, Lampman) which Stringer discusses in his short article. He queries the exact nature of Lampman's escape from the city and goes so far as to suggest that Lampman, perhaps, has already done his best work and that, given his limitations, is unlikely to do much more. This latter point is of some interest since it can be associated with a later debate of some standing about Lampman's early death and the resultant loss of what should have been, potentially, his most creative and accomplished period. Stringer, of course, was passing judgment—boldly or rashly —really on the basis of one book, *Among the Millet*.

A more theoretical approach to Lampman was to be expected, and we find evidence of this tendency in the short paper of A. W. Crawford. The writer is orthodox enough in that he sees Lampman as a nature poet with descriptive rather than interpretative interests, and we hark back to L. E. F. Barry's point about the absence of "man" from Lampman's poems. But Crawford also takes a new tack. He suggests that the poet is concerned purely with Beauty, and affirms, here, the legitimacy of a Keatsian connection, but he goes on to argue as well that while poetry may be the vehicle of Beauty, it should not be used as a vehicle for religion and philosophy. Finally, Crawford not only introduces the term "Ottawa School" into his discussion, but he also attempts, within the limits of his piece, what is probably the earliest systematic analysis of certain elements of Lampman's technique, rhythm, emotion and content.

By the time that John Marshall came to write his ambitious article on Lampman for *Queen's Quarterly* he had at his disposal a very substantial body of the poet's work which included the relatively recent "Collected Poems" of Duncan Campbell Scott's Memorial Edition of 1900. Marshall, it may be noted, had been a newspaperman, had taught school and was professor of language and literature at Queen's University. He edited annotated selections from Wordsworth and Longfellow, and was one of the editors of *Queen's Quarterly*. This background information may be of some significance because of the rather special slant which marks Marshall's article. In some ways it echoes that early preface of Andrew Shiels which lamented the poverty of Canada's past history, as well as the absence of suitable legends and the monuments of antiquity. The real argument, however, revolves around the issue of the quality of Lampman's poetry, and the stature of Canadian literature. The yardstick is to be found in the work of English poets and in the performance of English literature, and Marshall's quarrel with Lampman is that the poet works in imitation of worn-out old world themes while neglecting the source material of Indian tradition, the feats of the early explorers and the real potential of Nature. The call here is for a new criticism to guide the new literature of Canada and to warn against false directions. While Marshall makes several good points, the general tenor of his comments is essentially negative, and the impression is one of carping criticism which shows that Lampman had his critics who were as determined to find fault as his supporters were committed to displaying his strengths.

Untermeyer's essay is concerned primarily with Lampman as a writer of sonnets. It is an outside opinion which may be found, by some, to be a trifle disappointing if only because it shows no new or special insight into Lampman's work and simply substantiates the claim that the poet has been neglected unjustly, while attempting to explain his withdrawal into nature as a conscious rejection of fame and a turning away from men and their cities. But the emphasis is on Lampman and the sonnet, a form in which, Untermeyer believes, the poet is "at the very height of his genius." The analysis of several of Lampman's sonnets shows how the poet utilized the form for his own purposes. Here, once more, we note the Keatsian connection which Untermeyer discusses very briefly before concluding his paper with a curious mixture of praise and diffidence for Lampman's overall performance as a poet, and a singling out of certain patently unsuccessful poems as being "particularly noteworthy."

Lawrence J. Burpee was a civil servant, an honorary secretary and sometime president of the Royal Society of Canada, and a distinguished man of letters whose interests lay in the explorer era in the history of this country. In 1909 Burpee published a small volume entitled, *A Little Book of Canadian Essays*, which consisted of sketches of several Canadian writers amongst which was the present essay on Archibald Lampman. Burpee's paper is in interesting contrast to the earlier one of Marshall who, among other things, had accused Lampman of carelessness and ineptitude. Burpee—and in this he sides with the majority of Lampman critics—believes that Lampman was an unusually careful and accomplished craftsman. He goes on to argue that Lampman impresses with the polish and finished quality of his writing, and that his craftsmanship lies not only in the great care which he exercises in his choice of words, but also, in what Burpee identifies as an unusual instinct for language.

Bernard Muddiman's paper coincides, more or less, with the beginnings of modernism in poetry in the English language. And while one hesitates to suggest that Muddiman's essay is the signal of some kind of new critical approach inspired by the *dicta* of a new poetry and an emerging modern ideal, it must be noted that it is in Bernard Muddiman's essay that we can detect an important shift in taste and in what the critics consider to be good Lampman. For example, poems like "The Monk" which had been praised by Burpee and other early critics, and others like "The Vase of Ibn Mokbil" which had attracted Louis Untermeyer, had been assessed, by Muddiman's time, for their real worth. The change in taste was quite significant, so much so that the precious element of Keats which had been noted approvingly by earlier critics, would be recognized by Muddiman in terms such as, ". . . palpably modeled on Keats. . . ." The Keatsian echo will be picked up by other critics, and they too will consider it a weakness. There is general agreement though, that Lampman's good poems are really good, and "The Frogs," "Among the Timothy" and "Heat" are used frequently as examples of his skill. Muddiman suggests, though, that

Among the Millet is Lampman's best book, and that exactness of imagery was Lampman's greatest strength. It is also Muddiman who takes the important step of exploring the true nature of Lampman's debt to Keats. In this investigation he takes both poets back to the original, and, as it happens, to the common source of inspiration, classical Greek literature. Out of this probing of sources, Muddiman proposes that classicism is a spurious element in Lampman, and that Keatsian overtones in his poetry are inconclusive because Lampman tends to be Keatsian in language only without a corresponding element in his ideas or feelings. *Alcyone* and *Lyrics of Earth* are rejected by Muddiman as exhausted or played-out Lampman, and the assertion is made once more that the sonnet is Lampman's major claim to fame, while his chief weakness is identified as a lack of sensual love which could be seen as an extension of earlier criticism which had noted the absence of the truly human dimension in Lampman's poetry.

By the time that G. H. Unwin came to write his essay on Lampman, the collected poems had appeared in several editions, and Lampman was as established a poet as the Canadian scene would allow. A curious, new factor had come into its own in Canadian writing at this time. This factor was linked to what would be described today as popular culture, and it was making itself felt in the early decades of this century in the popularity and wide success of poets like William Henry Drummond and Robert W. Service. Unwin mentions this conflict between the appeal that could be hoped for in serious art, and the commercial success of Drummond and Service. But it is the scope and the all-embracing quality of Unwin's approach to Lampman which, in particular, distinguish this essay. Early in his discussion, Unwin agrees with most of his predecessors that Lampman's strength is in his nature poems and in the sonnets, and he asserts that poems such as "The Monk" are failures. But then Unwin becomes much more systematic in his evaluation of Lampman. He divides his discussion into individual appraisals of the three early books, and tries to develop connections with English literature, notably the connection with Wordsworth. He discovers a difference, however, in the use that Lampman makes of nature compared to that of Wordsworth. As Unwin has it, "Lampman's attitude toward Nature is primarily aesthetic. . . . There is, however, no attempt to establish a definite philosophy of life." According to Unwin, Lampman fails as a writer of long narrative poems but he is redeemed by the fact that he is always "true" to his material, and that he never strays far from reality or the actual fact. Oddly enough (as compared to earlier critics), Unwin sees Lampman as an interpreter, and compares him to Roberts whose talent is defined as chiefly descriptive. In the fourth and final section of his paper which has borrowed its subtitle, "Poems and Ballads," from the fifth section of Lampman's collected poems, Unwin addresses himself to what is probably the least successful part of Lampman's work as it stands presented in the Memorial Edition. Significantly, it is here that Unwin runs into difficulty (probably because of material like "Phokaia" and "The Vase of Ibn Mokbil") and, other than making the point that, "As a poet of humanity Lampman has not the direct contact with life . . ." and noting Lampman's indignation in "Modern Politician" and "To an Ultra Protestant"—both of which occur in the preceding section entitled, "Sonnets"—he is content to let his discussion rest with a tribute to "the essence of Lampman's genius."

With Raymond Knister's essay on Lampman we mark the beginning of a modern approach to the poet's work. It is an approach of which the question as to why Lampman did not become a great poet may very well be central as well as characteristic. Knister stresses with more than usual emphasis Lampman's tendency to eschew *man* in his poetry, and the corresponding preference for Nature. Knister is interested in solving this problem, and he concedes that Lampman's later writing "widened to include the major human emotions," but these at the same time are subject to those conscious controls which are the mainstay of Lampman's art. Knister's analysis of Lampman's poetry is whole and perceptive. He takes into account the idea of Canada as a setting for romantic adventure; the colonial overtones of Lampman's time; the cult of nature as literary tradition reaching from Rousseau, Goethe and Wordsworth; doubt and social indignation; escape and delight in the crystallizations of pure and external nature; gnawing reality and the spiritual force of imagination; and finally the iron hand which bated the lyric outcry, and checked the passion and the abandon of Lampman's statement. For Knister, as for others, Lampman's strength is in his "passion for exactitude in description," and in his uncanny feeling for words. while his achievement in the sonnet—a form with which he is most at home—is seen as truly great.

Leo Kennedy's shortish article on Lampman is part of a process current in the 1920s and the 1930s which was aimed at cutting the older poets down to size. The idea—in brutal terms—seems to have been one of attacking and whittling down the overly large reputations of poets of the preceding era in order to give the emerging poets of a new generation a chance to compete. As a result, Kennedy attacks "boosterism" which has made it possible for the old poets to stay "up there," and he displays that social pre-occupation which is characteristic of his time. Kennedy is critical of Lampman because Lampman does not live up to the socially extreme and politically committed expectations of the Thirties. In the light of this approach, Lampman is guilty of over-concentration on Nature, and, by inference, he is also guilty of disregarding the social and political reality of his age. The Kennedy article is interesting historically in that it represents an assault on lingering elements of Victorianism made by the modernists of the Twenties and Thirties. It must be noted as well, that the

Kennedy position is a near classic illustration in itself of the unthinking impatience and the consequent rejection by the movement of the Thirties of much of value that had gone before it. The central problem, perhaps, at the heart of the Kennedy piece is that Lampman is criticized for not writing in the 1890s in a manner which would have suited the 1930s. Much of the article, therefore, is querulous and polemical, and yet it stands as an important period-piece marked by a most illuminating closing paragraph.

In the instance of W. E. Collin, we have a contemporary critic who made two serious and elaborate attempts at a Lampman appraisal. The article which is reproduced in this collection became a preliminary study which was later expanded and developed into the forty-page essay, "Natural Landscape" which opens Collin's collection, *The White Savannahs* (1936). Several important points concern Collin in his paper as he undertakes his study of Lampman by first trying to place the poet in his literary context. He is particularly interested in the wellsprings of Lampman's creative impulse, and in the major influences working in the latter's background. Collin's approach is via an understanding of major themes in Lampman's poetry, and via a series of rather diffident textual soundings. He raises, as well, a consideration which has an important place in the contemporary discussion of Lampman. This has to do with the problem *cum* affliction of Ottawa's alleged provincialism. A condition which is supposed to have had considerable effect on Lampman's outlook and which, it is claimed, caused Lampman's spiritual and intellectual discomfiture. Collin is interested, as well, in the importance of the influence of Matthew Arnold, and he attempts an explication of "The City of the End of Things" as part of a general effort to trace the extent of Lampman's indebtedness to the English poet. In his discussion of "The City of the End of Things," Collin also advances the idea that the poem derives from Lampman's reading of Thomson's "The City of Dreadful Night," although he admits that this claim is based on general similarities between the two poems. The main thrust of Collin's thesis, however, is that Lampman's relationship with nature was based on the need for escape from a stifling provincial city; that Lampman's intellect was in danger of becoming moribund and that the poet fled into the country (both in fancy and reality) as the only escape and salvation available to him. Lampman's realism, then, becomes a kind of correlative here. Finally, but no less important is the point that Collin makes when he confirms earlier critics in their tendency to see Lampman as much more of a Hellenist than has been normally accepted.

The 1940s were an important period in Lampman criticism chiefly because Professor E. K. Brown had developed a profound interest in the poet's work, and was engaged in examining some of the surviving Lampman papers and manuscripts. The most important result of this interest and activity was the substantial essay chapter on Lampman in Professor Brown's study *On Canadian Poetry* (1943; rev. ed. 1947), and the publication of *At the Long Sault and Other New Poems* which came out in 1943. The three pieces under the signatures of Ralph Gustafson, D. C. Scott and John Sutherland which form a part of the present volume may be said to be related to this new and modest collection of some of Lampman's unpublished poetry.

Ralph Gustafson seems to be concerned with the problem of Lampman *versus* his environment, and thus becomes involved in trying to disprove Collin's assertion (also shared by E. K. Brown) that Lampman would have done immeasurably better had Ottawa proved to be a more stimulating city. Gustafson's position—so to speak—is that only the poem matters, and that much of the socio-historical context is not overly relevant. There are two particularly interesting points in the Gustafson essay. The first is that in arguing the relative unimportance of the Lampman/Ottawa issue, Gustafson had the benefit of the D. C. Scott letter which is included in this volume. Scott suggests that Lampman was as well off as one could have hoped (a point developed fully and admirably by Professor Beattie in his essay on Lampman in *Our Living Tradition,* First Series, 1957), and points to the need for a total re-assessment of Lampman's character and personality. It must be noted as well that there is no evidence that the Scott letter may have been helpful in getting Gustafson away from the problem of Lampman *versus* environment and on to a better tack which brought Gustafson's discussion to a sharper if narrower focus in the specifics of Lampman's poetry. The second point concerns Gustafson's uncanny reference to "the existence but not the plot of an intense personal drama." The traditional view has been that this personal drama at which Scott hints and which Gustafson recognizes, was a compounding of family tragedy. The death of an infant son, the agony of the terminal illness of Lampman's father, generally straitened circumstances combined with personal ill-health were all considered to be part of the explanation in this instance. There is more to the story, however, and Lampman's papers promise to throw light on emotional upheaval which, in turn, might lead to a fuller understanding of poems like "A Portrait in Six Sonnets." Another element which interests Gustafson is the significance of Lampman's hypochondria (see also Dudek's essay) combined with that paradoxical mixture of sweetness and sadness which marks certain of Lampman's poems. Gustafson suggests that Lampman was not too badly off, and that he was a poet who believed in the importance of what would be described today as "involvement." Gustafson goes on to argue ingenuously that Lampman's rejection of the world and the city, and by extension of Ottawa, was merely in compensation for his own inability to cope with life or to enter into it as fully as he would have liked. In the latter part of his paper, Gustafson takes issue with E. K. Brown's contention that the mature Lampman was moving into poems of "the

drama of life," and maintains that, on the contrary, Lampman had fled into abstraction.

The Duncan Campbell Scott letter of July 1945 which
is so useful in our understanding of Lampman's alleged
dilemma to say nothing of its being helpful in our reading
of the Gustafson essay, really requires no comment. It is
not only self-explanatory, but proves to be an important
document of Lampman criticism and biography.

John Sutherland's article on certain of Lampman's
poems is an intricate and elaborate attempt to cut Lampman and other Canadian poets down to size by proving
their derivativeness. It is particularly valuable to recognize
one of the bases of Sutherland's effort as being part of his
general quarrel with the imitative quality and values of
much of Canadian poetry. For Sutherland, literary colonialism and the colonial mentality in Canadian literature
were responsible for that sense of hopeless inferiority
which afflicted and affected Canadian writing. Lampman
happened to provide Sutherland with convenient examples
to illustrate this point.

In general terms it must be admitted that it is difficult
to arrive at a real evaluation of Sutherland's careful *tour
de force* of comparison and analysis which is the essence
of his paper. One suspects that most readers would grant
that Sutherland has made a case, but it is one which is as
elaborate as it is tenuous. However, "line by line" textual
analyses of Canadian poems are something of a rarity, and
Sutherland manages to be as intriguing as he is critical,
so that his paper complements a similar attempt at textual
appraisal of a Lampman poem by Desmond Pacey. Pacey
succeeds at one of the few known efforts at an *explication
du texte* of a Canadian poem. Appropriately enough his
subject is "Heat" one of Lampman's most successful
poems, and recognized as such from the earliest Lampman
criticism. Pacey's method speaks for itself. It moves surely
and convincingly about its task of uncovering the many
layers of image, rhythm, structure and mood which have

gone into the making of the poem. Yet, methodical and convincing though it is, one is left wondering if the "problem" of the last stanza of "Heat" is really solved or satisfactorily explained.

The last two essays in the present collection represent the kind of interpretative criticism which takes full account of the "given" of a writer's life and relates it to his circumstances and performance in order to arrive at a measure of the man, key elements in his writing, and the true nature of the society and ideas which informed his work.

Louis Dudek begins his examination of Lampman in the light of a comparison with the other poets of the Confederation Group, and goes on to point out that Lampman's significance is in that his concerns are related to the concerns of our times. Dudek suggests that Lampman's sadness and the *malaise* which apparently underlies his sadness are both due to ". . . the difficulty of the poet's position in a rudimentary and practical culture. . . ." The second important point made in Dudek's paper has to do with the ideational value of Lampman. Dudek's theory is that Lampman is not so much a poet of ideas as he is a poet of unresolved conflict or tensions (a point taken up by F. W. Watt as well). And the conflict, significantly enough, is between Wordsworthian and Arnoldian elements in Lampman's background and poetry. As far as nature is concerned and Lampman's escape into it, Dudek prefers to see nature in Lampman as an idealized concept and an idlyllic experience which cannot prove to be anything other than unreal. Nature, then, represents a romantic dream with which Lampman was probably quite uncomfortable. The corollary of romantic nature in Lampman's work is the real life of the city which Lampman views uncompromisingly, and records with a good deal of personal anguish. The failure of Lampman in the latter case, if it can be considered a failure, is one which is most likely to occcur in his philosophical poems. Dudek believes that Lampman is unable to penetrate to the core of social evil and to particularize the real demons of society, just as he avoids the expression of a direct and forthright pessimism. The weakness in Lampman, then, as perceived by Dudek is a basic ambivalance in his position, an ambivalence which makes his poetry ". . . one of unresolved tension and incomplete statement."

Professor Watt is somewhat differently pre-occupied. His concern is with an old problem in Lampman: the extent of the poet's commitment to nature, and the corresponding issue of Lampman's feelings about the city in which he lived and society around him. Watt attacks the problem by going back to an early parable-like piece of Lampman's prose, the fairytale "Hans Fingerhut's Frog Lesson." Professor Watt sees this as containing, possibly, the key to Lampman's spiritual and artistic dilemma. Here, alienation from the community is a central issue, although Watt suggests that the story shows the familiar pattern of the "hero's withdrawal from the world, his initiation into mysteries, and his return to society." Nature as a regenerative force and as the element holding the key to moral laws long lost to man is another theme which Watt examines. But the major pre-occupation of this essay is the opposition of the world of nature to the world of the city. Watt agrees with Dudek that Lampman's inability to participate in a full life created a fundamental uneasiness and tension in him which is revealed in Lampman's "city" poems. Watt believes, and here he runs contrary to Dudek's interpretation, that Lampman was not realistic, and that poems like "The City of the End of Things" were meant as symbolic visions. The remainder of Professor Watt's paper is concerned with a study of Lampman's attitudes towards urban civilization and its chief product the industrial city. In this sense Professor Watt places major emphasis on the "social" Lampman with his utopianism and the political overtones of community of ownership and brotherly love and co-operation.

MICHAEL GNAROWSKI

SOME RECENT CANADIAN POEMS

"FIDELIS" (AGNES MAULE MACHAR)

The people who are always asserting that we have no literature and no poets to speak of must take some trouble to avoid looking into volumes like that recently given to us by Mr. A. Lampman under the somewhat fanciful title *Among the Millet*, taken from the first poem in the book. Some of the poems in this volume have already appeared in American magazines, and in either Britain or the United States it would justly be considered the work of a true poet. And if it were unwise and unworthy of true lovers of literature to greet the effusion of our young Canadian Muse with extravagant laudation instead of discriminating criticism, it were both ungenerous and unpatriotic to withhold honour where honour is justly due.

No competent judge can examine Mr. Lampman's volume without feeling that it represents real work, as well as imaginative power, delicacy of perception and vivid faithfulness of description, as well as a high degree of general artistic excellence and careful technique. Mr. Lampman is not at his best in his lyrics, and we miss in these the fervour and force which George Cameron so specially possessed. His distinguishing excellence lies in his fine poetic thought, vivid description, grace and suggestiveness, and when he takes human life as his subject, he manifests a power and a pathos that promises still better things in the future.

From "Some Recent Canadian Poems," by "Fidelis" (Agnes Maule Machar). In *The Week* 6 (March 22, 1889), 251-52.

It is a pity we think that the volume had not a more characteristic title. The little poem, "Among the Millet," is a charming lyric, reminding us of a parable of Schiller's; but its five verses seem scarcely strong enough to bear the weight of seventy "other poems," many of them much longer, that make up the book. One of the strongest lyrics is the one entitled "What Do Poets Want with Gold?" though all might not be inclined to give the same answer, and it is unfortunately possible to starve out the muse as well as to over-feed her, and when Mr. Lampman tells us that

> The sweetest songs are sung
> Ere the inner heart is stung

we feel inclined to put in a query, to remind him of "Mary in Heaven," and of a well-known line that tells us that poets "learn in suffering what they teach in song."

In some of Mr. Lampman's longer descriptiveness we feel a certain unsatisfactoriness, as if, with all their beauty, the poems lacked an adequate *raison d'être*. We seem to ask for it a stronger motif. To stir us strongly the description of outward beauty needs a strong human or subjective interest, otherwise it seems only a sort of fragment such as the compass of a sonnet can best contain. In such poems as "Among the Timothy," "Winter," "Winter Hues Recalled," while there is true and delicate description, we miss something more, something which would have given the description a greater value. It strikes us like a noble portico which leads nowhither, or like an exquisitely carven frame which enshrines no picture. It is indeed a common tendency among some of the most popular poets of our day to fall into the old Greek habit of resting in "Nature," instead of fulfilling the nobler function of interpreter, without which Poetry is "divine poetry" no longer.

But we are far from meaning to say that Mr. Lampman is insensible to this deeper function of poetry, only that in some the description rather over-loads the theme. This is not the case in "April," which breathes the very spirit of that month of promise. We must stop to quote one verse:

> The grey song-sparrows full of spring have sung
> Their clear thin silvery tunes in leafless trees;
> The robin hops, and whistles, and among
> The silver-tasselled poplars, the brown bees
> Murmur faint dreams of summer harvestries;
> The creamy sun at even scatters down
> A golden green mist across the murmuring town.

In "The Frogs" the poet seems to us to fall into an opposite error. The occasion seems too slight to hang on it so much thought. There is imagination of a high order, beauty of diction, picturesque description and musical metre; yet we feel that the author has scarcely the right to read so much into the monotone of our "Canadian Nightingale." We may not be able to explain the reason why the song of the skylark is so different that Shelley's immortal lyric seems like its natural human equivalent. The poet carries us with him all through. But we can scarcely follow Mr. Lampman when he calls the frogs

> Breathers of wisdom, even without a quest

and tells us

> That earth, our mother, searching in what way
> Men's hearts might know her spirit's inmost dream,
> Ever at rest beneath life's change and stir,
> Made you her soul, and bade you pipe for her.

This was doubtless written in a mood when the author has dreamed himself into what he wrote, but we feel it too purely fanciful, and rather resent it as an attempt to carry our sympathy by a tour de force of charming imagery.

But when Mr. Lampman enters the domain of human interest we have few faults to find. Such a poem as "Between the Rapids" is altogether delightful. The scenery, the life of French Canada, is all about us as we read. We hear the "sudden, quickening roar" of the rapids, the bleat of the sheep, the "stilly rush of the low, whispering river," the "faint-heard song" or "desultory call." We see the "leafy mountain brow," the fields "all a blur" in the summer dusk, "the lowing cows whose shapes I hardly see." We seem to know the light-hearted Virginia, and are sure she is there still, and we seem to feel

> The cool wind creeps, the faint wood odours steal
> Like ghosts adown the river's blackening floor.

The mood of the voyageur is quite real to us—the momentary longing to stop and see the old home and the old home faces, and then the force of the restless spirit that bears him on with the swifter rush of the stream. For it is only between the Rapids. We have taken this poem in detail because it is a good example of the tenderness, sweetness, susceptibility to natural influences, delicacy of description and musical diction that are characteristic of Mr. Lampman's best work.

"The Little Handmaiden," "Abu Midjan," "The Organist," and "The Monk" are all graceful narrative poems— the two latter possessing much pathos. "Easter Eve" is tragic, but too hopeless in tone for a Christian subject, and "The Three Pilgrims" seems to us to have too much realistic horror for good art. It is undoubtedly strong, but the effect is simply harrowing, and the reader shrinks from reading it through.

In his sonnets Mr. Lampman is at his best. The form seems to suit him better than that of the simply lyric poem. Among those we specially like to dwell on are "Music," "Sight," "Knowledge," "In November," "The Lens" and the "Autumn Maples." We think the closing one scarcely a fitting winding up, however, for so good a collection. Much as we admire "the dog" himself, this particular specimen seems hardly worthy of a sonnet, or of being found in such choice company. It is an instance of an insufficient theme.

These poems have been already noticed in *The Week*, but they will bear a good deal of reviewing. They are not of the class that can be dismissed in a word as "meritorious verse," but are worthy of the careful appreciative study that we hope they will have from many readers in Canada and out of it.

PROMINENT CANADIANS—XXXV:
ARCHIBALD LAMPMAN

LILLY E. F. BARRY

In countries like the Motherland, ripe with honourable years, rich in illustrious ancestry, and still rapidly productive of individual types of greatness, a man must indeed be essentially a heroic figure—using the attribute in the sense which Carlyle attaches to it, in order to capture the attention and compel the admiration of a people long used to appraise merit in every form.

But in this young Canada of ours, we have less reason to view with indifference or apathy the efforts of a son of the soil to carve out for himself a noble career, the success of which must be of inappreciable value to his country, helping to invest her with a dignity which all her achievements hitherto, in the political, agricultural or commercial orders, have been powerless to obtain for her.

For a nation's patent of nobility is her poets' list. Not Alexander, but Homer, immortalized his country, Virgil is greater than Caesar; the land of Shakespeare takes precedence of the land of Wellington; the pen of Longfellow is mightier than the sword of Washington. It remains for Canada, or to be just, we should say English Canada, to produce her singers, before she can hope to be admitted into the aristocracy of nations.

Viewing her destiny in this light, it becomes apparent that any evidences of extraordinary talent, or to be bolder, let us say any promise of genius, on the part of her sons, must be eagerly looked upon by men imbued with national

"Prominent Canadians—XXXV: Archibald Lampman," by Lilly
E. F. Barry. In *The Week* 8 (April 10, 1891), 298-300.

spirit, as the possible germ of that intellectual greatness, without which mere material prosperity would be but a vain and barren result.

Though it might be rash and even dangerous to forecast the future of a man as young as Mr. Lampman, yet there are, in the work he has already produced, suggestions of power, insight, wisdom, pathos, courage and truth, which, in the mind of an attentive reader, breed hopes of a very high order indeed, and are, we think, a sufficient justification for the assumption that his success is a matter of national importance.

Granting this fact, no excuse need be offered for making his character and work a theme for serious study and public discussion, though a perfectly fair and frank treatment of the subject is as yet, for obvious reasons, a task of more than ordinary difficulty and delicacy.

.   .   .   .

Thirty years ago, namely, on the seventeenth of November, 1861, at the little post-village of Morpeth, in the county of Kent, and on the shore of Lake Erie, our poet, Archibald Lampman, was born. His parents though both Canadians by birth are descended from German families and people who love to ascribe the credit of a man's attributes to his ancestors will doubtless recognize, in our poet's contemplative disposition, a tendency inherited from his Teutonic forefathers, who flourished in the middle of the last century.

But during the hundred and fifty years or thereabouts which have elapsed since the old German stock struck root in transatlantic soil, it is more than probable that the radical change of conditions resulted in an entirely new variation of type, so that the poet of today may legitimately be regarded as a genuine Canadian product. A few years after the birth of his son Archibald, Mr. Lampman, who is a clergyman of the Church of England, was removed from Morpeth and appointed to the Parish of Perrytown, a

small village in the county of Durham, about nine miles
from Port Hope. The change proved disadvantageous in
many respects. The place was thinly populated, and its
surroundings bare of beauty or interest. After about a year
of residence, Mr. Lampman gave up his pastorate, and
brought his family, now consisting of a boy and three girls,
to Gore's Landing, on the shore of Rice Lake.

Here, at least, if other things were lacking, there was
compensation of a kind likely to be appreciated by the
dawning enthusiasm of an ardent lover of nature. It was
far from being a misfortune that the lad's fast developing
powers had no larger scope for exercise than the narrow
limits of this country village with its peaceful environs.
No doubt this circumstance did much to foster the habit
of patient and minute observation, which made the future
poet so fine a master in the art of description.

Concentration of his forces was more judicious than
expenditure as a preparation for the future. His range of
vision being narrow, his perception grew keen, his tastes
pure, his knowledge of things exhaustive. He came out of
this primitive school better equipped for intellectual
achievement than many a youth bred in the classic atmosphere of the university and subject to the stimulating
processes of foreign travel.

But though circumstances may have been in many
respects unfavourable to the advancement of the young
and earnest student, he was at least highly fortunate in this
that he found a large share of sympathy and encouragement under his own roof. Thus he enjoyed a happy immu-
nity from the sufferings which are the inevitable fate of a
sensitive nature, unsupported by watchful affection and
intelligent sympathy. His mother, herself a woman of
talent and taste, was eminently qualified to understand the
bent of her son's mind, and to assist him in developing the
spiritual forces latent within him. Her indomitable courage and perseverance succeeded in overcoming every
obstacle that lay in the way of her son's education. The

best tuition available in the country was secured to him, and happily it was not long before the fruit of her noble endeavours began to appear.

In 1876, the young Archibald was sent to Trinity College School, Port Hope, where he rapidly distinguished himself, and ended by outstripping all his comrades. He then entered Trinity College, Toronto, where he won several scholarships and finally took his bachelor's degree in arts with honours.

During his three years' sojourn there, he may be said to have been initiated into the secrets of the Literary Guild by assuming the editorship of the college paper. Many of his first published efforts, both in prose and verse, appeared in its modest columns, and his reputation as a poet soon became firmly established among his immediate friends and acquaintances.

Upon leaving college, Mr. Lampman went to Orangeville, where he accepted the post of Assistant Master of the High School. His duties there proving uncongenial, they were given up in the course of a year, and Mr. Lampman removed to Ottawa, where he received an appointment in the Post Office Department which he still continues to hold.

It is scarcely to be supposed that it is in the nature of a poet to take kindly to the daily routine of office drudgery. Indeed, one could well imagine the writer of such lines as:

> Oh, for a life of leisure and broad hours
> To think and dream, to put away small things

and,

> For life, this joyous, busy, ever-changing life
>   Is only dear to me with liberty,
> With space of earth for feet to travel in
>   And space of mind for thought. . . .

throwing down his misused pen in despair at the end of a day's prosaic official duties, with the heart-wrung apostrophe to Fate: "Let me make the songs of my country, and I care not who makes her postal regulations."

Yet it is by no means to be feared that the interests of the Department suffer at the hands of Mr. Lampman, for he is a thoroughly conscientious worker at any task.

Only we can not but hope for a future happy condition of things which shall raise him above the necessity of common labour, and give him free scope to exercise the nobler faculties with which he can best serve his own and his country's interests.

Mr. Lampman's marriage to Miss Maud Playter took place in 1887, and has proved, in the truest sense of the usually conventional phrase, a "happy event." But into his domestic life we may not look too curiously. It is enough to know that the same kind Fate which surrounded his earlier years with a woman's devotion and sympathy has made similar provision for the larger needs of his later life. The dedication lines of his book, *Among the Millet*, would alone convey to the world a strong enough hint of the harmonious influences at work in the poet's home. The epigram of compliment does not often cover such a subtle, tender feeling as has inspired those two exquisite little stanzas.

Previous to the publication of his first collection of poems, Mr. Lampman's frequent contribution to *The Week*, and to several American magazines of high standing, had secured for him an attentive and appreciative circle of readers. But it was not until the appearance of his book *Among the Millet* that he reached the dignity of a recognized master of his art. Favourable notices of the work appeared in the best reviews. Distinguished pens put forth their dicta on the excellence of his performances, and people who had hitherto never heard of the young poet became curious and looked first idly then eagerly into his poems. The book had a good sale and gained a wide reputation for its author.

Upon him, now, the eyes of many are turned in hopeful

expectation of still greater things than he has yet accomplished. Shall he be one of the select few whose work already points strongly towards our literary independence, and promises to create for us a Supreme Court of Appeal in the order of letters? It may not be, yet we are inclined to believe that whether or not he accomplish his part of this great work is only a question of his enduring fidelity to the mission upon which he has embarked.

Possibly, too, the reception he meets with may have a determinative influence on his success. We, being comparatively a young people, are not yet so perfectly attuned to the divine harmonies of poetry that we can catch their strains and intercept the beauty of them as they float by us half drowned in the busy hum and roar of the homelier arts. We think we would like to have poets; indeed, we know that we must have them, and yet we do not rightly understand the nature of our duty to them once we have got them.

We are children into whose hands a beautiful and complicated piece of mechanism is placed as a gift. Obviously our first duty is one of study. If we are willing to accept a man as a teacher, we must place ourselves on a footing of affectionate familiarity with his works. To begin with, his books must be our own. A hasty perusal of a borrowed volume counts for absolutely nothing in the province of study. We must suffer it to lie near our hand, and acquire a habit of looking into it at odd moments, comparing our impressions with the author's, correcting our own if necessary, turning his wise words well over in our mind, until their meaning becomes perfectly mirrored in our intelligence, until we can apply his maxims to the test of our every day experience. Then, and only then, our duty to the man who wrote it has been fulfilled. The reward of such calm and patient study will follow in due order and become abundantly manifest to our consciousness in various ways.

.   .   .   .

One's first impression of Mr. Lampman's poetry is a delightful sense of its freshness. The turn of thought is original, the phrase choice and unhackneyed, its burden a continuous revelation of beauty, peace, order and undisguised beneficence.

The simplest theme tempts his facile pen as well as the noblest. He skilfully assimilates the most trivial seeming details of a landscape into his finest descriptions, transforming them by his treatment into valuable bits of local colour. Here are a few instances from the poem on "Heat." The italics are mine.

> By his cart's side the waggoner
> Is slouching slowly at his ease
> Half-hidden in the *windless blur*
> *Of white dust* puffing to his knees.

> From somewhere on the slope near by
> Into the pale depth of the noon
> A wandering thrush *slides leisurely*
> *His thin revolving tune.*

> The grasshoppers spin into mine ear
> *A small innumerable sound.*

> In the *sloped shadow of my hat*
> I lean at rest and drain the heat.

Here are vivid pictures drawn with a single stroke from material which, to the average writer, would seem utterly void of inspiration. Familiar sounds, too, are reproduced with startling accuracy:—

> The restless bobolink loiters and woos
> Down in the hollows and over the swells,
> Dropping in and out of the shadows,
> Sprinkling his music about the meadows,
> Whistles and little checks and coos
> And the tinkle of glassy bells.

The book teems with similar instances of Mr. Lampman's happy descriptive power. From the seen to the un-

seen he passes with facility, forging the fetters of his verse
for both with equal success:—

> Weary of hope that like a shape of stone
> Sat near at hand without a smile or moan.
> That aching dim discomfort of the brain
> Fades off unseen, and shadowy-footed care
> Into some hidden corner creeps at last
> To slumber deep and fast.

His secret of discovering the most charming resem-
blances and analogies lends another charm to Mr. Lampman's descriptions. Here is an exquisite example:

> The daisies that, endowed
> With stems so short they cannot see, up-bear
> Their innocent sweet eyes distressed, and stare
> Like children in a crowd.

And again:

> Across the unfenced wide marsh levels where the dry
> Brown ferns sigh out and last year's sedges scold
> In some drear language rustling haggardly
> Their thin dead leaves and dusky hoods of gold
> Across grey beechwoods where the pallid leaves unfalling
> In the blind gusts like homeless ghosts are calling
> With voices cracked and old.

The use of such strong imagery produces a powerful
effect on the mind of the reader. It peoples the woods and
meadows for him with a life that is almost human, and
interests him to fascination. It compels him to habits of
close observation and awakens within him something of
the ardour which stimulates the poet in his constant quest
of beauty.

Away from nature's own haunts, Mr. Lampman's talent
does not desert him. He turns to the haunts of men and
finds:

> The bell-tongued city with its glorious towers,

the city that:

> Strains with its eternal cry

the railway station where

> "Ever on" my blinded brain
> The flare of lights, the rush, and cry, and strain,
> The engine's scream, the hiss and thunder smite
> I see the hurrying crowds, the clasp, the blight
> Faces that touch, eyes that are dim with pain:
> I see the hoarse wheels turn, and the great train
> Move labouring out into the brownless night.

Passing from the descriptive to the more purely didactic poems, Mr. Lampman reveals to us another facet of his diamond-cut intellectuality. For a man so young in years, the maturity of his thought, the calm wisdom of his utterances, the austere morality of his principles, fill us with astonishment, nay we might even say disappoint us, in a measure. We naturally expect to find symptoms of the hot blood of youth, with traces of its generous errors, its unconscious foolish pride, its naive self-complacency, its airy miscalculations, its oblique judgments, in the written sentiments of a man under thirty.

But in all these respects Mr. Lampman has kept himself above reproach. He has given us no confession of weakness, direct or tacit. If at times he, like his fellows, becomes conquered by a mood that is not lofty or a sentiment that is not noble, he wisely refrains from yoking such lapses to the working of his muse which he reserves for the highest service only.

His poems, on the whole, though strongly marked with his individuality, are decidedly impersonal. His soul is of the convex order. It loves to diffuse its own light and is careless about concentrating upon itself every visual ray within its focus. The humility of true greatness is amply revealed by this self-elimination and contrasts favourably with the tone of complaint and revolt common to young writers.

Assuredly there is at times in some of the poems an unmistakable undertone of wistful regret for the prisoned fate of the liberty-loving spirit, but this is by no means akin to the penseless ravings of shallower minds against the unpropitious environment of circumstances, and is far from vexing the general serenity of the poet's even temperament. He accepts life as he finds it, and leaves the madness of attempting to re-make the world to fools who have no better task in hand.

Between the rocks of passion and pride Mr. Lampman steers his poetic bark with unceasing vigilance, keeping equally wide of the heat of the one and the blindness of the other.

The poems that treat of love are delicately pure. It is a tender, brooding, protecting love they describe, a love that hallows its object, which could never under any circumstances defile it. Thus:

> Yearning upon the faint rose-curves that flit
> About her child-sweet mouth and innocent cheek,
> And in her eyes watching with eyes all meek
> The light and shadow of laughter, I would sit
> Mute, knowing our two souls might never knit;
> As if a pale proud lily-flower should seek
> The love of some red rose, but could not speak
> One word of her blithe tongue to tell of it.

If it were not too long, I should like to quote the whole of the lovely poem "Before Sleep," as a further illustration of this exquisite trait. The *embarras du choix* prevents one from selecting any particular passage out of the perfectly charming whole. Let the reader look for it in the text; it more than repays perusal.

As there is no coarseness of sentiment, neither is there any undue haughtiness of judgment in Mr. Lampman's strongest expression. There is observable in poems of a certain cast a degree of just indignation, excited by the consideration of error, of vileness, of what in a sense is still worse, the blind stupidity of unthoughtful men:

> Grey children who have madly eat and drunk
> Won the high seats or filled their chests with gold
> And yet for all their years have never seen
> The picture of their lives, etc.

But there are no displays of impotent anger, no wholesale denunciations of life and society, intellectual fireworks which splutter and go out leaving the last darkness worse than the first. Mr. Lampman is not alone a man of acute sensibility; he is supereminently a man of sense. He affects no lofty superiority to the rest of mankind. He has a sense of brotherhood for all, of which the law is one of love, not cold disdain. Of the poet he says:

> He must walk with men that reel
> On the rugged path, and feel
> Every sacred soul that is
> Beating very near to his,
> Simple, human, careless, free,
> As God made him, he must be.

And here is a passage, which methinks recalls a master, whom to name with Mr. Lampman would only do violence to the modesty of the latter. Perhaps the reader may surmise who I mean:

> How beautiful is gentleness, whose face
> Like April sunshine, or the summer rain
> Swells everywhere the buds of generous thought
> So easy, and so sweet it is; its grace
> Smoothes out so soon the tangled knots of pain.
> Can ye not learn it? Will ye not be taught?

Of the five or six narrative poems which the book contains, the simplicity and pathos of "The Organist" will no doubt please the greater number of Mr. Lampman's readers, and make them wish there were more of the kind. Indeed, if we had a reproach to make to Mr. Lampman, it would be his fondness for the same class of subjects, the same moods and grooves of thought. We are convinced it is by no means from poverty of resource that his poems are chiefly the result of long and lonely contemplations, and in consequence uniformly serious, meditative, austere. We would like to see more of the exuberance of youth, with its extremes of joy and pain, its laughter and its tears. We want to be stirred up with stories of strong effort, high hopes, and their attendant excitement, and above all we clamour for pictures from the humorous side of life. A man is never wholly our friend until we have laughed with him. He cannot be considered wholly a genius until he has found his way to our hearts through all the avenues of sensibility.

I am far from implying that Mr. Lampman is lacking in a sense of humour, but I believe if he would indulge it more frequently, he would appreciably shorten the distance between himself and his readers. Now such passages as this we would gladly see multiplied:

> Like a flight of silvery arrows
> Showers the sweet gossip of the British sparrows,
> Gathered in noisy knots of one or two,
> To joke and chatter just as mortals do
> Over the day's long tale of joys and sorrows;
> Talk before bed-time of bold deeds together,
> Of thefts and fights, of hard-times and the weather,
> Till sleep disarm them, to each little brain
> Bringing tucked wings and many a blissful dream,
> Visions of wind and sun, of field and stream,
> And busy barn-yards with their scattered grain.

This is perfectly charming. A physiogonomy of cast-iron should smile at this irresistible picture of the private life of these little winged scavengers reviewing the incidents of their day's "fights" and "thefts," "hard-times and the weather."

To many readers the "Sonnets" will prove the most attractive portion of Mr. Lampman's book. They are like beautifully moulded crystals, through which the living though imprisoned thought shines radiantly forth. There is a completeness and raison d'être about each one which efface all marks of the care and industry which must have gone to the making of it. Mr. Lampman will not be over-ridden by Pegasus in the field of sonnet-writing; he has caught the bridle and mastered the steed, and now leads him hither and thither as his fancy wills.

The wealth of the universe, the beauty of life, the large-ness of knowledge, the joy of love, the pain of doubt, the darkness of despondency, the sweetness of sympathy: these are among the fruitful themes his muse has dealt with and sweetly discoursed upon. And the burden of it all is one of good cheer, of noble consolation. There is no word or sug-gestion of despair in the whole book; not a drop of spleen, not a breath of sin. And yet, it is quite as happily free from virtuous cant or commonplace morality. It is, in a word, the product and exponent of a great soul, a gentle heart, a refined taste and a pure life. It is a book of much meaning, merit and dignity, and takes its place, as a matter of course, among the best works of our best writers.

Since the publication of his first collection of poems Mr. Lampman's activity has by no means diminished. Contri-butions from his pen are being constantly solicited by the best magazines in the country, and the supply seems equal to the demand.

Doubtless, too, Mr. Lampman is reserving his best efforts for a second volume; considering the ease with which he writes, it ought to be forthcoming in a year or two. Its evidence will be required to shape the general verdict con-cerning the value of his influence. If it fulfils the promise of the first, his fame will be firmly established not only as a poet but equally as a patriot. His gallery of Canadian landscapes can do more for the popularization of our land than any merely political or commercial agitation. His accession to the dignity of a master would stimulate national sentiment in proportion as it lessened our obligation to go abroad for a respectable authority in matters of literary taste and judgment.

The high state of finish which characterizes all Mr. Lampman's compositions, and the purity of his English, free from provincialisms or mannerisms, amply justify the hope that he may eventually challenge comparison with some of our best English writers. This is the

Consummation devoutly to be wish'd

by all true Canadians. Nothing less can wholly satisfy us at the present stage of our history.

I trust that in confining myself to the limits of my subject, I shall not seem to have wilfully ignored other writers of consequence who have already gained distinction as poets of no mean order. Their names come readily enough to the lips of Canadians whenever there is question of growth of national literature, and to me, as well as others, represent a high order of talent, and are associated with many delightful hours of private study. There has been no attempt in the foregoing lines to make invidious comparisons. To assert the pre-eminence of one over the many who have already become famous, or who are fast making for celebrity, would perhaps be a rash and even unjust proceeding. Individually, thoughtful readers have no doubt formed their own conclusions regarding the matter. Time alone can settle the verdict for all.

A GLANCE AT LAMPMAN

ARTHUR STRINGER

So much has been written and so much has been said concerning Canadian literature, that there are many who are beginning to doubt the existence of such a thing—contending that if a literature really exists in Canada, it would not be necessary to indulge in the prevalent, and perhaps too blatant, trumpeting of our heretofore necessarily meagre accomplishments. An earnest and patriotic, but, at the same time, an unhappy attempt, has been made to "boom" our literature. Like all "booms" it has proven unsatisfactory and unprofitable, fatuous and illusory. We are beginning to realize that to scream at one another that we have a literature is not going to give us one. We are beginning to see that this state of self-consciousness is hampering and confining; that it cannot admit of literary freedom and activity. And to that voice that comes from time to time across the sea, asking in tones of mingled reproof and entreaty why we have not a national literature, we can only sadly but hopefully reply:

We have many promises, many blossoms that should betoken much fall-time fruit. We can only wait, and if, after all, the day of national literatures is not over and gone, we may give you something with the flavor of a great land of great lakes and mountains and plains, that will smack piquant in the cloyed stomachs of your trans-marine gourmands.

It is undeniably true that there are many promises of Canada some day possessing a number of strong and healthy literary characters; but too much trust should not

"A Glance at Lampman," by Arthur Stringer. In *Canadian Magazine* 2 (April 1894), 545-48.

be placed in mere promises. In his "Victorian Poets," Stedman disposes of the Canadian contingent in six lines, I believe, devoted to one poet and only one.

It would be both foolish and elusive to expect to see suddenly spring up, like mushrooms, a horde of Canadian writers and poets; it is enough to hope that our schools and colleges may take advantage of the fresh, sturdy material they have to deal with, and turn out men fit for sound intellectual and literary work. So far, they have failed to do so.

It was little more than courtesy that prompted an American poet, when with us not long ago, to say there was something in this Canadian air of ours that made poets. But everything should not be left to the air. In this age, our colleges and universities have their part to do; but I doubt which is the most potent of good results, the Canadian air or the Canadian university.

There is one strongly marked characteristic of the existing generation of Canadian poets—that is, intense seriousness. They have, perhaps unfortunately, little or nothing of the humor found in contemporary American versifiers; but they have an earnestness and a loftiness of ideal that is sadly lacking in much American verse. Mingled with this they have the freshness of a young race, and the strength of a northern one. It may be that this loftiness and high endeavour is, as yet, a comparative failure; but the soul is there, and the technique is a thing that can be acquired. But when there is no soul, all the technique under the blue heavens is only a mockery.

Of the group of Canadian poets who have obtained a recognized standing—Roberts, Lampman, Carman, Campbell and Scott—probably Lampman is the most thoroughly Canadian and in Canada the most popular. He is not as scholarly as Roberts; he has not the strong imaginative power of Campbell; he may not have the mysterious melody of language peculiar to Carman, nor the pleasing

daintiness and occasional felicitousness of Scott; but he is
the strongest and broadest poet of the group, possessing the
most of what Landor has called "substantiality." He has an
artist's eye for color, and the quiet thoughtfulness of a
student for scenery—the true nature poet. No one has
written more happily of our seasons and landscapes of the
long, white, silent winter; of the warm, melodious awakening spring, of the hot, parched, Canadian mid-summer
days, with their dust and drought, and of the reddening
and yellowing leaves of autumn, that most sorrowful,
though beautiful, of all seasons in Canada, when summer
wanes, and the birds fly southward, and the rime comes on
the fields, and finally snow and silence dwell on the barren,
desolate, wintry earth.

I can readily understand why God put man on His
world. Without humanity the most beautiful world is an
unreal dream; beauty exists only when man exists to call
it beauty; and things are not what they are but what we
make them. Without thought, nature is nothing. That is
an old, well-worn saying that in the world there is nothing
great but man, and in man there is nothing great but
mind; but its age and its repetition only intensify its truth.
Lampman says:

> Why do ye call the poet lonely,
> Because he dreams in lonely places?
> He is not desolate, but only
> Sees, where ye cannot, hidden faces.

The poet is he who sees—a more difficult thing than
humanity imagines. We say the poet's fancy, or imagination, or dreams, casts prismatic hues about what he sees,
but, in reality, this fancy is the essence of truth, just as
prismatic hues are the essences of white light, unrevealed
until the prism analyses the colorless ray and shows its real
elements. In the same way as the prism, the poet acts in the
truths he gives forth, showing that they have something

more than their apparent elemental white light, that they, too, have their violet and blue and orange and red.

But Lampman sees nature in a peculiarly simple light; there is little of the transforming fancy in his word-painted scenes. They are more real than ideal. I do not mean that Lampman is what is called "a realist"—what poet could be one?—for after reading a poem like "The Frogs," in which an apparently realistic and commonplace subject is idealistically treated, such a supposition becomes impossible. The poet establishes a strong bond of sympathy between men and those dreamy pool-bubblers, the frogs:

> Breathers of wisdom won without a quest,
> Quaint, uncouth dreamers, voices high and strange,
> Flutists of lands where beauty hath no change
> And wintry grief is a forgotten guest;
> Sweet murmurers of everlasting rest,
> For whom glad days have ever yet to run,
> And moments are as atoms, and the sun
> But ever sunken half way toward the west.

> *   *   *   *   *   *   *

> Morning and noon midnight exquisitely
> Wrapt with your voices, this alone we knew,
> Cities might change and fall, and men might die.
> Secure were we, content to dream with you,
> That change and pain are shadows faint and fleet,
> And dreams are real and life is only sweet.

It is the poet who finds the latent beauty in what the world thoughtlessly passes over as prosaic or repulsive. Who ever before thought there was so much sentiment connected with that little, neglected, abused, serio-comic animal—the frog?

Lampman is a town man who likes to leave the fret and fever of the city and wander out into the quiet country, find a pleasant or a striking landscape, and then examine and absorb it. Having done this, he reproduces, with faithful minuteness, the scene, and it is in reproduction that one is impressed with his power of delineation and unerring detail. It is accurate and suggestive, graphic and impressive. None but a true artist could write the following lines; they are more than the work of a mere craftsman:

> Beyond the dusky cornfields, toward the west,
> Dotted with farms, beyond the shallow stream,
> Through drifts of elm with quiet peep and gleam,
> Curved white and slender as a lady's wrist,
> Faint and far off out of the autumn mist,
> Even as a pointed jewel softly set
> In clouds of color warmer, deeper yet,
> Crimson and gold, and rose, and amethyst,
> Toward dayset, where the journeying sun grown old
> Hangs lowly westward, darker now than gold,
> With the soft sun-touch of the yellowing bows
> Made lovelier, I see, with dreaming eyes,
> Even as a dream out of a dream, arise
> The bell-tongued city with its glorious towers.

But for the obtrusiveness of that lady's wrist—but for that little straining for a back-ground figure, the picture is a perfect one.

What reader has not felt the power of the poem called "Heat"?

> From plains that swell to southward, dim,
>   The roads runs by me white and bare,
> Up the steep hill it seems to swim
>   Beyond, and melt into the glare.
> Upward half way, or it may be
>   Nearer the summit, slowly steals
> A hay-cart, moving dustily
>   With idly-clacking wheels.

One can see that crawling hay-cart with the vividness of a picture; one can almost feel the quiver of the hot midsummer air, and smell the dry, hot dust.

By his cart's side the wagoner
   Is slouching slowly at his ease,
Half-hidden in the windless blur
   Of white dust puffing at his knees.
This wagon on the height above,
   From sky to sky on either hand,
Is the sole thing that seems to move
   In all the heat-held land.

Very much in the same excellent style is "Among the Timothy," where

The crickets creak, and through the noonday glow,
   That crazy fiddler of the hot mid-year,
The dry cicada plies his wiry bow
   In long-spun cadence, thin and dusty sere;
From the green grass the small grasshoppers' din
   Spreads soft and silvery thin;
And ever and anon a murmur steals
   Into mine ears of toil that moves alway,
The crackling rustle of the pitch-forked hay
   And lazy jerk of wheels.

To any one who has been in the hay-field and has heard the "crackling rustle" of the dry hay, and the jerk of the moved-on wagon wheels, the power of Lampman's pictures must strongly appeal.

This poet is a healthy child of nature, nursed by that broad, strong mother, the innocent earth. Happily he has none of the morbidness to be found only too easily in several young Canadians: grey children grown old in their youth. With Lampman, the smiles were ever too near the lip for him to make his life discordant with his own words, when he said:

Poets speak of passion best
When their dreams are undistressed,
And the sweetest songs are sung
Ere the inner heart is stung.

Emotion and melody seem mingled, like sunlight and cloud, in the sonnet on "Music":

> . . . calm and yearning undersong,
> Now swift and loud, tumultuously strong,
> And I in darkness, sitting near to thee,
> Shall only hear, and feel, but shall not see,
> One hour made passionately bright with dreams,
> Keen glimpses of life's splendor, dashing gleams
> Of what we would, and what we cannot be.
> Surely not painful ever, yet not glad,
> Shall such hours be to me, but blindly sweet,
> Sharp with all yearning and all fact at strife,
> Dreams that skim by with unremembered feet,
> And tones that like far distance make this,
> life
> Spectral and wonderful and strangely sad.

The due proportion between language and thought is likewise in nearly all of Lampman's work. He seldom relies on illegitimate artistic effects. There is so much that is good in him; there is so much that is worth quoting—that it is difficult to do him justice by tearing out a few tattered stanzas. But I must be content with one more quotation—a few lines from "Aspiration":

> Oh deep eyed brothers, was there ever here,
> Or is there now, or shall there sometime be
> Harbor or any rest for such as we,
> Lone, thin-cheeked mariners, that aye must
> steer
> Our whispering barks with such keen hope and
> fear
> Toward misty bournes across that coastless sea,
> Whose winds are songs that ever gust and flee,
> Whose shores are dreams that tower but come
> not near.

Archibald Lampman is often spoken of as a young man to be measured by his promise more than by the greatness of his accomplishment; but it seems to me he has done his best work and has risen to his greatest height. He has felt his limitations. But this accomplished work is so excellent for its kind, his art is so pure and chaste, that we cannot be but well satisfied with what he has done. If he has still better work in store for us, it will be a surprise, but an agreeable one. It would be foolish to expect anything more thoroughly Canadian, for Canada at present is hardly in a condition for poets to grow enthusiastically patriotic over; and while patriotism in itself is a good thing, the poet who loses himself in rapturous expressions of our national glory could not be considered otherwise than very imaginative and very nonsensical, and perhaps he who thinks Canadian literature is anything more than the trans-frontier radiation of a central luminary, be it England or America, is likewise imaginative and nonsensical.

ARCHIBALD LAMPMAN

A. W. CRAWFORD

The materials which flow to the hands of the poet in this country are almost prodigious in extent. Poets, perhaps, above all men love nature, and revel in her mysteries and her beauties, and here we have nature in her grandest costumes, the varied magnificence of her summer robes and the simple purity of her winter garments. We have lakes, rivers, and waterfalls, rocks, hills and mountains, prairies and wooded lands, and happy is the man whose earliest years have been associated with some of these places. A

"Archibald Lampman," by A. W. Crawford. In *Acta Victoriana* 17 (December 1895), 77-81.

richer heritage no man can have, for these will be to him "a thing of beauty" and "a joy forever." And there is no Canadian scarcely but has this glorious heritage, this inspiration toward beauty. Consequently it is only natural that we should have a school of nature poets springing up in one of the finest parts of this Canada that knows nothing but magnificence, and from ocean to ocean and from the lakes to the end of the earth is one constant inspiration to the poetic mind.

Thus we have the Ottawa School, called from the fact that they are situated at the capital, but the term Lake School would be scarcely less appropriate than it was to that famous school of which England feels so proud. And as one of the foremost poets of this school we have the subject of our present writing, Archibald Lampman, a name known and esteemed throughout both Canada and the United States.

The writers of this school, as is implied in the very fact of grouping them together, possess many qualities in common, and in our characterization of Lampman's poetry, we will necessarily give an account of some qualities which may be just as fairly stated of any of the members of this school, or of any Canadian poets for that matter, but we will try to make our divisions narrower as we proceed, that we may finally come to consider the qualities held by him distinctively.

There has been made a classification of poetry into poetry of Art and poetry of Energy, or, as these have been termed by others, the poetry of Creation and the poetry of Self-expression. Now, in order to see this clearer, we might take as the representative of the first class, John Keats, and of the second, Mrs. Browning, not to say that either of these is lacking in the qualities of the other division, or that true inspiration is lacking in either, but only that above all others these qualities are prominent. To the class of the poets of Art, Lampman belongs. He is gifted with a considerable amount of Energy, but his Art is supreme.

His poetry ofttimes is brilliant by reason of its polish, rather than by reason of the inward fire which brightens and gives form to the whole structure. We might say that his is the poetry of Reflection, rather than of Inspiration, if we do not use these terms in too extreme a manner. We find him giving very little self-expression, in the proper sense of the word. He does not unveil for us the hidden workings of his own heart and life. We might read through almost his entire work, and know nothing about him but the thoughts he has had concerning things outside himself.

And so we see another feature of his work: Objectiveness rather than Subjectiveness. The great ebb and flow of feeling that may be in his own soul he scarcely reveals to us. He does not deal with the thoughts which primarily arise within and which he afterwards sees objectified or illustrated by the outward world, but with those which primarily have to deal with the outward world and which that world has given him concerning itself. It is impossible to say which is the higher kind of poetry; and perhaps it is scarcely proper for us to strive to place one above the other, but only to say that they are equally high, their relative importance depending upon the skill of the poet using them; a happy combination of both, however, being preferable to either one in a distinctive way.

Another feature of his objective art is, that it is mostly concerned with Nature rather than Man, which perhaps is one of its weaknesses. True, the highest art, viz., the dramatic art, is essentially objective, but it is man in his objective aspects rather than nature. Shakespeare's art is objective as scarcely any other's is. It so fully covers himself that from his dramas we can scarcely pick out a single thought or feeling that belonged to Shakespeare the man. Yet he dealt almost entirely with man, as his art demanded, and not with nature. And Keats, whose art, although not dramatically developed, was almost next to Shakespeare's, was necessarily objective, but not of nature alone; it is concerned with nature as it is connected with man. In fact, poetry of nature is valuable only as it brings nature into connection with the human soul, thus showing the essential unity of all nature. Lampman has, however, shown himself quite capable of thus dealing with man, and it is shown quite as well in his beautiful poem, "The Organist," as in any other of his productions. This is perhaps the best executed of all his poems, containing a large element of emotion.

We may also add that his poetry is concerned chiefly with Beauty, and this is always the primary purpose of true art. Poetry's first business is to give pleasure, and this can be done only through Beauty, and the poet who forgets this, or whose nature causes him to neglect it, will win the reward of his neglect by passing into oblivion, though he may flourish for a time among pious or other minded people. Lampman's poetry is instinct with Beauty. Its very life is Beauty, and he breathes in an atmosphere of Beauty. But that is not all. He is essentially ethical and religious, and no line of his having a contrary quality has ever come under our eye. He has not that sturdy, robust faith of a Whittier, but that supreme regard for everything good and true which characterized Keats. Beauty, then, with him is primary, as it should be, and "Among the Millet," may be taken as a representative poem, giving the key-note of all his writings. Poetry as the vehicle of Beauty is legitimate, but poetry as the vehicle of Religion and Philosophy per se is quite illegitimate.

There is one feature which we would not expect to find, considering he is an earnest student of Wordsworth, and that is that his concern with nature is Description rather than Interpretation. Wordsworth is the great interpreter of nature, and it seems scarcely to be an end in itself; but with Lampman, Nature seems herself his goddess, and he worships her for her own sake. Not to say that he does not interpret nature, but that he is oftener a describer of nature. He sees his conceptions and thoughts in Nature herself, not in her as the garment, or as the illustrator of some other world of thought and feeling. This reminds one of Byron, who, thinking Pope the greatest of poets, yet could not write a line like him, but whose lines were always Byronic, not Popian.

Now, having tried to determine his particular sphere as a poet, let us turn for a brief consideration of his more specific qualities as these are manifested within that sphere, or rather shall we say, to his relative development of these qualities which must in a greater or lesser degree belong to every poet.

I think we are safe in saying his Individuality is not strongly marked. We might see a great many of his productions and not be able to tell to whom they belonged, any more than to say that they belonged to some member of the Ottawa School. This is not a defect, when we consider them to be all young men who have no doubt done only a small portion of the work allotted to them, and when we consider the restraints placed upon modern orthodox magazine poetry. Individuality of life and of work are usually the result of progress and evolution. All men start at nearly the same place, and their individualities are shown more and more as they advance, and not till they advance. Perhaps, however, there are not many essential diversities in the genius of the different members of this school, and their distinctions from other schools will be more marked than distinctions among themselves.

We notice that he uses a great many different stanza forms, creating them to suit his varying purposes. He has a great deal of skill in handling and in originating these, and is not bound by the hard and fast lines of ordinary forms, but freely uses what suits his purposes. The Sonnet, however, is his favorite form, and in this he has done his most excellent work, and it, no doubt, will be a permanent addition to the literature of the English language. It is difficult to find any more excellent in the literature of today, and those entitled "A Prayer," "Knowledge" and "Light," are especially worthy of mention.

Looking at his Rhythm, we find it often somewhat harsh and artificial. His lines occasionally look like things which are made, and not things which exist in their own right and have a life inherent in them which gives them form and color. There should be a reason for the existence of everything, and for its existence in its particular form, but this perhaps is impossible to discern in all his poetry. There are, however, a great many lines which seem to stand out from the general structure as particularly beautiful and rhythmical.

His Emotion is perhaps as deficient as any quality and no quality exerts a stronger influence on all the varied forms of poetry than emotion. A rhythm born of emotion will live in its own right, and be natural and clear, and suited to the connection as part of an organism. His poem entitled "The Organist" will doubtless be seen to have as much feeling as anything, and is truly a noble creation. It will show the fact that emotion will find its own rhythm, much better than any mental analysis could give.

In this, also, his imagination is quite equal, if not superior, to anything else he has written. In "The Monk," the imagination is good, but the execution is scarcely as good as in "The Organist," where we see excellent imaginings, the work of that faculty which brings the divine into the horizon of the human, and raises the human into the region of the divine.

In the brief space at our disposal we cannot analyze any closer, but may just remark that when we apply to his writings the higher tests of poetic genius, spontaneity, sweep, intellect and imaginative power, he will be seen to compare well with anyone in the range of Canadian literature, and we believe that when the great temple of Canadian fame shall be built, he will have a chief place among the elect; and no matter how great a place the literature of Canada may occupy in the history of the world, still he will be seen to have an enviable position, and his writings a permanent place in our literature.

ARCHIBALD LAMPMAN

JOHN MARSHALL

Grant Allen, I think it was, maintaining once that there was a plethora of talent in England, placed the number of contemporary poets at sixty, many of whom, he admitted, however, were unknown beyond the circle of their friends and admirers. A recent volume of Canadian essays discusses "the works" of sixty "well-known Canadian poets," twenty-two "French-Canadian authors, churchmen and statesmen," and eighty-five "Canadian women writers," no name occurring twice, as might be expected, in this rather illogical classification. It was the difficulty, presumably, of enumerating all our writers of prose that left the classification incomplete as well as illogical. Had our able editors, war correspondents and what not been included, the list of Canadian literary men and women might easily have run up into hundreds. It is pleasant and patriotic, no doubt, and apparently not inconsistent with the form of imperialism current amongst us, to think that we, who have recently given the mother country pointers in campaigning and shown her the strength of that imperial sentiment whose existence her Cobden clubs and Manchester politicians had denied, can surpass her also in the sphere of intellect and art. In these matters unfortunately, however, patriotic feeling is not entirely to be trusted. It is apt to be a little over-enthusiastic, a shade too intent on utterance and too impatient of form, a trifle deficient in balance and measure, a little blind to the larger vision of humanity. The patriotism for example that believes in forming our children's minds on:

"Archibald Lampman," by John Marshall. In *Queen's Quarterly* 9 (July 1901), 63-79.

> We'll lick the Boer
> And wipe the floor
> With the enemies of the Queen,

or that persists in attributing to "the soldiers of the Queen," all the results of English energy, honesty and justice, however useful and necessary as a political force, is not the safest guide to calm and reasoned literary appreciation.

Literary excellence is not yet common and abundant even in Canada. On the contrary, "strait is the gate and narrow is the way and few there be that find it"; or, as the pagan poet long ago expressed it, "excellence dwells among rocks hardly accessible, and a man must almost wear his heart out before he can reach her." We all possess more or less imagination, otherwise the enjoyment of literature would be limited to its producers. In these days of universal education, moreover, the number is considerable of those who have sufficient command of the mechanics of verse to be admitted to the magazines. But the average editor is not exactly a poetical Rhadamanthus, nor is poetry quite identical with smooth rhythms, facile phrases and pretty sentiments largely derivative. What distinguishes poetry from verse-making is its consummate justness, its perfect balance, its unerring felicity, its "sweet reasonableness." In Shelley's fine phrase, poetry is "the record of the best and happiest moments of the happiest and best minds." When a thought has caught the poet's imagination and been dwelt upon—and only a worthy thought can thus compel attention—until its full significance is revealed and there has clustered about it a wealth of happy fancy and apt illustration, and when the thought thus touched, beautified, and made effective by emotion, has been uttered with power to excite like emotion in reader or hearer, we have poetry. What at any time we have ourselves felt of noble aspiration, poetry sets in shining lines, with perennial power of recalling those feelings so delightful, so elevating, but with us so evanescent. It not merely convinces the intellect but touches the heart. In the animation of mind and the bracing of the will, which it is thus the function of poetry to produce, the acceptance becomes easier of the otherwise bald and repellent truth, or the rule of life hitherto held irksome or arbitrary. Poetic power is, in fact, so rare a gift that in the whole history of literature scarcely a dozen persons have displayed it pre-eminently.

In thus setting our standard for poetry high we must of course be careful to overlook nothing of real merit however small. Indeed, its very rarity and worth should make us welcome any gleam of poetic truth and beauty. We must not, like the melancholy Jaques in "As You Like It," as described by Rosalind, "disable all the benefits of our own country, be out of love with our nativity and almost chide God for making us that countenance we are." In other words, we must not condemn poems or authors merely because they happen to belong to our own time and country. The distant is not really more interesting than the near. The past has no necessary monopoly of what is noble and heroic. In literature, as in other departments of human achievement,

> All experience is an arch, wherethro'
> Gleams that untravelled world whose margin fades
> Forever and forever when I move.

But to praise immoderately and without discrimination, to call that excellent which is only middling or even inferior, to give the rank of poet to men who are scarcely even smooth versifiers is to destroy all belief in excellence or desire for it in both reader and writer, and to prolong in consequence that very literary mediocrity against the charge of which we so indignantly protest.

Various restricting conditions have rendered rather abortive as yet the seeds of literary genius, which of course are sown in Canada as elsewhere. First there is the apparent lack of inspiring theme. The country is young. It is without historic halo. It has no antiquity, no legends, no impressive monuments, no places hallowed by the memory of heroic achievement, no noble architecture past or present. Everything seems new, raw and somewhat pretentious. The poetry reading public again is small and not very discriminating. Excitable enough, Canadians are deficient in imagination and emotion. Part are intensely practical, while the smart set, imitating the externals of English civilization, identify culture with certain conventional ways of speaking and behaving, with dress, equipage and manners. Neither are capable of an affection for so ideal and disinterested a thing as genuine poetry. What flatters their prejudices or prepossessions they applaud, the rest is moonshine. The lovers of poetry, few and scattered and somewhat ashamed of their "namby pamby" want of strenuousness, are for the most part incapable of appreciating the structure, the architectonics, as well as the sweetness and melody of a great poem. Our poets in consequence have a vague and cloudy understanding of their mission. Indisposed or unable to compose sustained and original works they keep turning out faint copies of European models. Meanwhile there remains unsung the poetry of the new world—the rapidly fading Indian tradition, the French missions, the voyageurs, pioneering, lumbering, the vast forests, great lakes and mighty rivers—and they will remain unsung, and our poets will continue to turn out ballads, canzonets, madrigals and reveries in imitation of the affectations of European poetry gone to seed, until a just and disinterested criticism has arisen, capable of performing the double service of warning our young writers of talent against false and unprofitable lines of work and creating for them by exposition and analysis an atmosphere of culture, an intellectual situation of which they can avail themselves. What musical criticism, within the last hundred and fifty years has done for Germany, making the Germans, not naturally gifted that way, the most musical

people in the world, literary criticism might do for
Canada. At any rate until there has been a more thorough
popularization of the great masterpieces of poetry we need
look for no native poetry of any considerable weight or
power.

I have been led by the laudatory essays referred to above
to re-examine the works of perhaps the least futile of our
Canadian writers of verse, Archibald Lampman, in the
complete edition brought out by Morang after the poet's
death in 1899. One lays aside the volume with a stronger
impression than ever of the derivative character of Lampman's work, his lack of originality, his narrow range of
thought and feeling and the almost entire absence of any
evidence of progress towards clearer and more consistent
views of life and art. His poems reveal neither the stages in
his soul's history nor any large organizing ideas round
which, as in the great poets, they group themselves. They
are merely the isolated expressions of more or less limp
and languid moods, begotten rather of reading than of
observation or reflection. Instead of the unique and inevitable phrase which no one else could give us, faint echoes
and fragments of various voices reach our ears.

No one familiar with Swinburne's "Deserted Garden"
and its morbid haunting melody, will have difficulty in
tracing the lyrical inspiration of the "Ballade of Summer's
Sleep":

> The woods that are golden and red for a day,
> Girdle the hills in a jewelled case,
> Like a girl's strange mirth ere the quick death slay
> The beautiful life he has in chase.

"Winter Hues Recalled" is plainly reminiscent of Wordsworth's "Prelude of Excursion":

> But in the east the gray and motionless woods,
> Watching the great sun's fiery slow decline
> Grew deep with gold. To westward all was silver.
> An hour had passed above me; I had reached

The loftiest level of the snow-piled fields,
Clear-eyed, but unobservant, noting not
That all the plain beneath me and the hills
Took on a change of colour, splendid, gradual,
Leaving no spot the same; nor that the sun
Now like a fiery torrent overflamed
The great line of the west. Ere yet I turned
With long stride homeward, being heated
With the loose swinging motion, weary too,
Nor uninclined to rest, a buried fence,
Whose topmost log, just shouldered from the snow,
Made me a seat, and thence with heated cheeks,
Grazed by the Northwind's edge of stinging ice,
I looked out upon the snow-bound waste,
The lifting hills and intersecting forests,
The scarce marked courses of the buried streams,
And as I looked lost memory of the frost,
Transfixed with wonder, overborne with joy.

We have here something of the movement of Wordsworth's ponderous blank verse, something of his occasional
garrulous enumeration of unvital and insignificant details,
with a tendency peculiarly the writer's own to wander
from the subject, that is to say, from colour to form, but
without any of those "gleams like the flashing of a shield,"
which so abundantly illumine Wordsworth's pages. At
another time it is the influence of Keats, a poet whose
method, according to his biographer, Lampman carefully
studied, that is most apparent. Compare the first stanza
of Lampman's "April":

Pale season, watcher in unvexed suspense,
Still priestess of the patient middle day
Betwixt wild March's humoured petulance
And the warm wooing of green kirtled May,
Maid month of sunny peace and sober gray,
Weaver of flowers in sunward glades that ring
With murmur of libation to the spring.

with the opening lines of Keat's "Autumn":

> Season of mists and mellow fruitfulness
> Close bosom friend of the maturing sun,
> Conspiring with him how to load and bless
> With fruit the vines that round the thatch eaves run,
> To bend with apples the mossed cottage trees,
> And fill all fruit with ripeness to the core.

Lampman's

> Dreaming of Summer and fruit-laden mirth

with a line from Keat's "Nightingale":

> Singest of Summer in full-throated ease.

Lampman's

> Quite forgot
> The shallow toil, the strife against the grain,
> Near souls that hear us call but answer not.
> The loneliness, perplexity and pain.

with Keats'

> Quite forgot
> What thou among the leaves hast never known
> The weariness, the fever and the fret,
> Here where men sit and hear each other groan.

or the following description of gnats from "April":

> the thin
> Mist of gray gnats that cloud the river shore,
> Sweet even choruses, that dance and spin
> Soft tangles in the sunset . . . .

with a similar description in the "Ode to Autumn":

> Then in a wailful choir the small gnats mourn
> Among the river sallows borne aloft
> Or sinking as the light wind lives or dies.

Picturesque epithet, syntactical arrangement, personifica-
tion, the use of apostrophe, the rhythmical movement and,
with modifications, the stanza form have all been derived
from Keats. Lampman's eye, obviously, being rather on
his author than on his object, with the inevitable consequence of loss of force and sincerity and occasional positive
absurdity as in

> Sunny glades that ring
> With murmur of libation to the Spring,

where the requirements of sense have been ignored for
the sake of rhyme and epithet. His manner, moreover,
varies not only from poem to poem, but from stanza to
stanza in the same poem. The grave and stately movement
of the opening stanza of "April," quoted above, suited to
the large, clear, objective treatment of the theme intended
in the poem, shifts in the second stanza with comical
abruptness into the peculiar cadence of curious antithetical
and fanciful introspection quite inconsistent with the tone
of the context:

> As memory of pain, all past, is peace
> And joy, dream-tasted, hath the deepest cheer.

Such imitative exercises in the style of their predecessors,
have been practised of course even by the great poets; but
whereas they have invariably gone on, their preliminary
experiments over, to conquer a style of their own, Lampman never acquired the unique and distinctive mark of a
master. His more characteristic work, if such it may be
called, exhibits the same want of individuality, the same
wavering and uncertain manner. A poem very much
praised by his admirers is "Morning on the Lievre."

> Far above us where a jay
> Screams his matins to the day,
> Capped with gold and amethyst
> Like a vapour from the forge
> Of a giant somewhere hid

Out of hearing of the clang
Of his hammer, skirts of mist
Slowly up the woody gorge
Lift and hang.

Softly as a cloud we go,
Sky above and sky below,
Down the river; and the dip
Of the paddles scarcely breaks,
With the little silvery drip
Of the water as it shakes
From the blades, the crystal deep
Of the silence of the morn,
Of the forest yet asleep;
And the river reaches borne
In a mirror, purple gray,
Sheer away
To the misty line of light
Where the forest and the stream
In the shadow meet and plight,
Like a dream.

From amid a stretch of reeds
Where the lazy river sucks
All the water as it bleeds
From the little curling creek;
And the muskrats peer and sneak
In around the sunken wrecks
Of a tree that swept the skies
Long ago,
On a sudden seven ducks
With a splashy rustle rise,
Stretching out their seven necks,
One before and two behind,
And the others all arow,
And as steady as the wind
With a swivelling whistle go,
Through the purple shadow led
Till we only hear their whir
In behind a rocky spur,
Just ahead.

Poetry there is here no doubt—the clear depths and mirror-like surface of the river winding through the primeval forest, the misty distances, the reflections in the water, the freshness of the morning, the feeling of solitude, the sensation as of floating in the air. But the form is in no necessary or organic connection with the thought. The diction is not happily inspired. It is without imaginative content. There are no phrases to startle by their unique inimitable charm and linger in the imagination long after. No fairy fancies, as we might expect from the subject, "ring little bells of change from word to word." The syntactical arrangement especially in the last section is ludicrous. The first image is inconsistent not only with itself but with the morning stillness. The reflection on the tree's having swept the skies long ago, has no connection with the thought of the poem. The bobbing rhythm, monotonous, unmelodious, wanting in subtle harmonies or delicate cadences, is grotesquely inappropriate to the theme, especially the, alternately plaintive and jerky, short line. The choice of details is poor and the arrangement still poorer. The poem has no proper beginning or end. It should have started with the second section, "Softly as a cloud we go." The scream of the jay should not have been introduced till after the flight of the ducks. As the poem deals with some of the evanescent effects of morning it might have occurred to the poet that the lifting of the mist and the shining out of the sun, changing, as it would, the complexion of the scene, might appropriately have been placed at the end. In that way the poem would have had a full and natural close. As it is, it merely stops. How much finer, in a somewhat similar picture, is Scott's choice and arrangement of details, how much more appropriate his rhythm:

> The Summer dawn's reflected hue,
> To purple changed Loch Katrine's blue;
> Mildly and soft the western breeze
> Just kissed the lake, just stirred the trees,
> And the pleased lake like maiden coy,

Trembled but dimpled not for joy;
The mountain shadows on her breast
Were neither broken nor at rest;
In bright uncertainty they lie
Like future joys to Fancy's eye.
The water-lily to the light
Her chalice reared of silver bright;
The doe awoke and to the lawn
Begemmed with dew drops, led her fawn;
The grey mist left the mountain side,
The torrent showed its glistening pride;
Invisible in flecked sky
The lark sent down her revelry;
The blackbird and the speckled thrush
Good morrow gave from brake and bush,
In answer coo'd the cushat dove
Her notes of peace and rest and love.

Lampman, according to his biographer, preferred to be judged by his sonnets. Like all distinct art forms, the sonnet is great support to a weak writer. It gives him a framework for his thought, while its length seems to impose no severe strain on his invention. The magazines are continually publishing so-called sonnets that deceive (so powerful is the influence of form) not only the careless public, but the authors themselves, with an appearance of hitting the mark. But really to hit the mark, to make a triumphant success in the sonnet, is to prove oneself no mean craftsman. To mold into perfect form within the narrow limits of fourteen lines, some weighty head, heart and hand. Whatever affectation, weakness or insincerity there is in a man's make-up is sure to appear, the student of poetry knows, in his management of the sonnet. It is a severe test, but to the sonnet let us go. Probably as favourable an example as one could choose of Lampman's sonnets, is that entitled, "Stoic and Hedonist":

The cup of knowledge emptied to its lees,
Soft dreamers in a perfumed atmosphere,
Ye turn, and from your luminous reveries
Follow with curious eyes and biting sneer

Yon grave-eyed men to whom alone are sweet,
Strength and self-rule, who move with stately tread,
And reck not if the earth beneath your feet
With bitter herb or blossoming rose be spread,
Ye smile and frown and yet with all your art,
Supple and shining as the ringed snake,
And all your knowledge, all your grace of heart,
Is there not something missing from your make?—
The thing that is life's acme and its key—
The Stoic's grander portion—Dignity.

The first line is applicable rather to the sceptic than to the hedonist, unless Lampman's hedonists, like Tennyson's lotos-eaters, plume themselves on the superior insight which has shown them that all strenuous effort is vanity. In any case its connection is not sufficiently clear, nor is it a satisfactory opening line. The second line expresses, not unsuccessfully, the hedonist's love of sensuous ease. "Luminous" attributes too much real light and imagination to selfish and sensuous dreamers. "Biting sneer" is inconsistent with "curious eyes." The connection of the line "And reck not if the earth beneath your feet" is ambiguous. It is applicable both to the hedonists and to the stoics. Its position points to the latter; "your" points to the hedonists who are addressed. If we substitute "who" for "and" and "path your brothers tread" for "earth beneath your feet," and let the line follow "Soft dreamers, etc.," there is, I think, a decided gain in clearness and power. "Smile and frown" is grotesquely antithetical; "grace of heart" is inconsistent with the character of the hedonist, as already sketched, and is obviously the result of a desperate search for something to fill out the line, and at the same time rhyme with "art"; "make," "acme" and "key" are all quite infelicitous. To venture too far out of one's proper sphere of criticism into that of construction is to court humiliation, but:

                            I am in blood
Stepped in so far, that, should I wade no more,
Returning were as tedious as go o'er.

For "biting," substitute "subtle"; for "sweet," "dear"; for
"move with stately tread," "contemptuous of ease"; for
"frown," "mock"; and for "atmosphere"—but I cannot be
expected to furnish rhyme and structure as well as criticism. Rearrange as follows:

> Soft dreamers in a perfumed atmosphere
> Who reck not if the path your brothers tread,
> With bitter herb or blossoming rose be spread,
> The cup of knowledge emptied to the lees;
> Ye turn and from your luminous reveries
> Follow with curious eyes and subtle sneer
> Yon grave eyed men to whom alone are dear
> Strength and self-rule, contemptuous of ease.
>
> Ye smile and mock, and yet for all your art,
> Supple and shining as the ringed snake,
> And all your knowledge, all your grace of heart.
>
> Is there not something missing from your make?
> The thing that is life's acme and its key,
> The Stoic's grander portion—dignity.

While still unpoetical the rearrangement is much superior
to the original in structure. Each quatrain has now its
peculiar office or function and so has each tercet. The first
quatrain describes the hedonists; the second, their contempt for the stoics; the first tercet, their grace and art;
and the second, their want of dignity. A composition that
admits of being thus treated, like a school boy's exercise,
can hardly be called inspired work.

    Tested on his own chosen ground, Lampman once more
turns out to be colourless and incoherent, lacking in
breadth and imagination, without individuality, infelicitous in expression, and wavering and uncertain in the

evolution of his thought. The failure of a writer to develop a distinctive manner of his own is proof of mediocrity. In no dilletante or art for art's sake sense, style is the essential thing in literature, and carries the rest along with it. It is the element of individuality, the note of sincerity, the measure of emotional depth and fervour. The thinker—scientist or philosopher—discovers new ideas. It is the business of the poet to make them prevail, to utter them persuasively, tellingly, to take the best ideas current or available in his time, suffuse them with feeling and out of them make beautiful and effective works of art. Poets are not touched but to fine issues. If a writer has only a languid interest in his theme, he is apt to be merely repeating other men's phrases. When thoroughly in earnest his style must be his own. It need not be absolutely flawless. A perfect harmony of thought and expression is possible only to a few. Of the vision and the faculty divine, the Wordsworths have more of the vision, the Tennysons rather more of the faculty; but, marred or flawless, a writer's style must have, for effect, a unique and personal quality. Style is never acquired by mere imitation. It is the reward of sincerity. The touch of truth and earnestness is the touch of life. Lampman put study enough on his art, but he had not ideas enough and he was not, in a literary sense, sufficiently sincere. His range of thought and sympathy was remarkably narrow. He had not the saving sense of humour which kept Shakespeare and Burns sweet and hopeful in spite of their clear perception of the errors and follies of men. The past does not seem to have interested him. The present bred only weariness and disgust from which he sought escape in domestic affection and the contemplation of nature. A sonnet addressed to his wife, shows more genuine feeling than anywhere else appears. But whatever consolation he obtained from nature is strangely incommunicable to his readers. He has neither Scott's eye for colour and variety, nor Shelley's vivid sense of the unity underlying all difference in nature. Tennyson's minute and delicate landscapes are as much beyond him as Byron's picture of nature's broader and mightier aspects. His handling of natural theme consists for the most part, as in the oft praised "Heat," of an enumeration, —lacking, as may be inferred from what I have already said of other poems, in architectonics,—of what may possibly have been significant to himself but which he fails to make vital to any one else. He has none of Seton-Thompson's love of animals, a single sonnet of no great merit, containing, I think, his whole contribution on that side. He has no rustic types—no Michaels, no Lucy Grays, no Highland Girls, no Solitary Reapers, no poems that one would take the trouble to memorize, nothing that could for a moment be placed alongside of "Fidelity," "The Reverie of Poor Susan," "To a Skylark," "She Was a Phantom of Delight," "Daffodils," or a hundred others that will occur to any reader of Wordsworth.

Imaginative but uncritical and over-generous readers invariably tend to add to the mediocre poet's work the gleam that never was on his performance. But criticism is concerned not with what the poet might do if your imagination amend him, but what he can do by his own sheer power of persuasion. Take, for example, Lampman's last poem, "The Largest Life," a title which, by the way, illustrates his want of sureness in the use of words.

I.

I lie upon my bed and hear and see
The moon is rising through the glistening trees:
And momently a great and sombre breeze,
With a vast voice returning fitfully.

Comes like a deep-toned grief, and stirs in me,
Somehow, by some inexplicable art,
A sense of my soul's strangeness, and its part

In the dark march of human destiny.

What am I, then, and what are they that pass
Yonder, and love and laugh, and mourn and weep?
What shall they know of me, or I, alas!

Of them? Little. At times as if from sleep,
We waken to this yearning passionate mood.
And tremble at our spiritual solitude.

II.

Nay, never once to feel we are alone,
While the great human heart around us lies;
To make the smile on other lips our own,
To live upon the light in others' eyes:

To breathe without a doubt the limpid air
Of that most perfect love that knows no pain:
To say—I love you—only, and not care
Whether the love come back to us again,

Divinest self-forgetfulness, at first
A task, and then a tonic, then a need;
To greet with open hands and best and worst,

And only for another's wound to bleed:
This is to see the beauty that God meant,
Wrapped round with life, ineffably content.

III.

There is beauty at the goal of life,
A beauty growing since the world began,
Through every age and race, through lapse and strife,
Till the great human soul complete her span.

Beneath the waves of storm that lash and burn,
The currents of blind passion that appal,
To listen and keep watch till we discern
The tide of sovereign truth that guides it all;

So to address our spirits to the height,
And to attune them to the valiant whole,
That the great light be clearer for our light,
And the great soul thus stronger for our soul:

To have done this is to have lived, though fame
Remember us with no familiar name.

Readers, whose own quick conception acts readily upon a
hint, catching here a glimpse of a fine idea and ignoring in
grateful enthusiasm the confusion and redundancy that
attend its expression, call this a beautiful and inspired
poem. The thought is certainly an inspiring one—the satisfaction resulting from going along with, rather than
counter to, the divine order that seems to be intended
and aimed at in the world, and from doing all we can "to
enlarge and increase the volume of the human stream
thitherward." Feebly or insincerely felt, however, and in-
sufficiently illuminated with ideas, the conception is
worked out in a sonnet sequence on the Shakespearean
model. Everyone knows the Shakespearean sonnet—three
quatrains developing the thought and leading up to a
consummation or climax in the couplet, some novel application or summing up of what has gone before. For its
successful handling, are required largeness of vision, poise,
intensity, a copiousness which permits of condensation and
compression. To attempt a sequence of three such sonnets
with a pinch of inspiration insufficient for one, is inevitably to fall into diffuseness, vagueness, incoherence,
bombast. Where thought is deficient there will be padding;
where feeling is languid, and elevation is attempted, there
will be affectation; where affectation and redundancy are
present, obscurity and incoherence result. Will any one
say that the flatness of many of the lines, and the false
note, the sepulchral solemnity, of the first sonnet, is not
the result of want of intensity or of simulating an emotion

not sincerely felt; that the diffuseness, the irrelevant details, the repetition of the same thought in other words, particularly in the second sonnet, are not owing to the necessity of filling three sections of fourteen lines each; or that the incoherence of the first, both internally and in its relation to the thought of the whole, does not come from the concurrence of vague thinking and languid emotion. The poem suggests, rather obviously I think in the connection between the first and the two following sonnets, the famous passage in "Tintern Abbey":

> For I have learned
> To look on nature, not as in the hour
> Of thoughtless youth; but hearing oftentimes
> The still, sad music of humanity,
> Not harsh nor grating, though of ample power
> To chasten and subdue. And I have felt
> A presence that disturbs me with the joy
> Of elevated thoughts a sense sublime
> Of something far more deeply interfused,
> Whose dwelling is the light of setting suns,
> And the round ocean and the living air,
> And the blue sky and in the mind of man;
> A motion and a spirit that impels
> All thinking things, all objects of all thought
> And rolls through all things.

But so far from Lampman's being disturbed by Wordsworth's elevated joy or sense sublime, so far from his poem's having peculiar power to lighten "the burthen of the mystery, the heavy and the weary weight of all this unintelligible world," so far from its tone's anywhere rising much above the level of prose, the whole might be rewritten as prose not only without loss of energy but even with added force and persuasiveness from eliminating those faults of redundancy, obscurity and affectation not tolerated by good prose. Compare with this, Tennyson's "Early Spring," a poem written at the age of seventy-five and dealing with the converse of Lampman's thought, the ideas of the dual operation of divine creative energy renewing and reviving the outer world of nature and the inner world of human thought and emotion.

I.

Once more the Heavenly Power
    Makes all things new,
And domes the red-plow'd hills
    With loving blue;
The blackbirds have their wills,
    The throstles too.

II.

Opens a door in Heaven;
    From skies of glass
A Jacob's ladder falls
    On greening grass,
And o'er the mountain walls
    Young angels pass.

III.

Before them fleets the shower,
    And burst the buds,
And shine the level lands,
    And flash the floods;
The stars are from their hands
    Flung thro' the woods.

IV.

The woods with living airs
    How softly fann'd,
Light airs from where the deep,
    All down the sand
Is breathing in his sleep,
    Heard by the land.

V.

O follow, leaping blood,
　　The season's lure!
O heart, look down and up
　　Serene, secure,
Warm as the crocus cup,
　　Like snowdrops pure!

VI.

Past, Future glimpse and fade
　　Thro' some slight spell,
A gleam from yonder vale,
　　Some far blue fell,
And sympathies how frail,
　　In sound and smell!

VII.

Till at thy chuckled note.
　　Thou twinkling bird,
The fairy fancies range,
　　And lightly stirr'd,
Ring little bells of change
　　From word to word.

VIII.

For now the Heavenly Power
　　Makes all things new,
And thaws the cold, and fills
　　The flower with dew;
The blackbirds have their wills,
　　The poets too.

But happily Tennyson has been inspired by his idea! Long past the time when other men sink into second childishness and mere oblivion, Tennyson has lost neither his sense of the eternal novelty, freshness, significance of the world nor his power of revealing it to others. With what beautiful art he selects the details that not only best present the concrete picture of spring but keep the reader constantly aware of the nearness and omnipresence of divine creative power, and, when we fancy the theme exhausted, with what surprised delight we watch its unexpected blossoming into the thought of the power of spring to revive in old age the feelings of youth, to germinate the dormant seeds of imagination so abundantly sown in the spring-time of life. Nor, with all his joyousness, is Tennyson too terribly at ease in Zion: a noble thought sincerely and profoundly felt is the source of a buoyant, yet deeply earnest tone. Both poems deal in different ways with the unity of man and nature. But while Lampman's is weak, diffuse, pensive as if with the touch of age, Tennyson's has the invincible hopefulness and the inexhaustible vigor of immortal youth.

Lampman's poetry rather sadly illustrates the impossibility of important or fruitful creative work until we have "a national glow of life and thought," the result of a more honest and more wide-spread critical effort than has yet been attempted in Canada. While the desire of his admirers to see him ranked with Wordsworth is absurd, Lampman had a genuine, though slender, vein of poetry. The shyness, the shrinking sensitiveness and delicacy of which his friends speak, and which one fancies he can see reflected in his portrait, are of the poetic temperament. To the development of his talent, however, not strong enough to make a way for itself, circumstances of education and subsequent life and environment were unfavourable. The son of an Anglican clergyman, he had, indeed, early access to the great literary models of the past, as well as the help and guidance of a man of no inconsiderable culture. But unfortunately he was sent to that type of school which tends, I cannot help thinking, to make gentlemen at the expense of a freeplay of thought, to check spontaneity and to over-emphasize respect for form, authority, convention.

From Trinity College School he passed to Trinity University, and thence, after a very brief and very unsuccessful trial of school teaching, to Ottawa and the civil service. It may be that the social and political life of the capital affords more than usual opportunities for observing human life on its shallower, weaker and meaner sides, but for such studies Lampman had no taste. "Once more," he tells us in "April," and again and again he repeats this in other words "the city smites me with its dissonant roar." From the "hot heart" of the city, he loved to pass to the wide spaces and green silence of nature and, while, as I have tried to show, he only fitfully and occasionally conveys to others a gleam of that illumination which he himself received, I have not the slightest doubt that he often entered a heaven shut to other men, to adapt Browning, "entered and took his place there sure enough though he came back and could not tell the world."

ARCHIBALD LAMPMAN AND THE SONNET

LOUIS UNTERMEYER

Archibald Lampman—to a few only do the words call back uncertain memories of various fugitive poems published in the leading American magazines some twenty years ago. These few will remember him, not for his message or the intensity of his purpose, but for the pathos and the broken beauty of his voice—a voice that ceased while the song still trembled on his lips. Shortly after his fatal illness, in

"Archibald Lampman and the Sonnet," by Louis Untermeyer. In *Poet Lore* 20 (November 1909), 432-37. By permission of the author.

February, 1899, Morang & Co. of Toronto, issued a memorial edition of his works—a noteworthy volume of some five hundred pages, including his three former publications; and the young Canadian poet, who had never heard the world's praise during his life, began to gain the usual tardy recognition. He was not a poet of the library—of midnight mythology and the smoking lamp; he was a poet of spring meadows, of budding orchards and of wild and grassy spaces. And he sang of the timothy and the comfort of the fields: of snowbirds and the summer's sleep; of hepaticas and forest moods; sang as a boy might carol in his dreams or a happy peasant might sing to the world. But the world is an ungrateful audience—its silences are disapproving and its applause is always ill timed. None felt this more keenly than Lampman himself, and as his voice grew surer and his powers wider, his singing concerned itself less and less with the stress and complexity of modern life; ceased almost to reflect the moving panorama of the crowded days and echoed only the themes of solitude and woodland wonders.

Nature in all her manifestations held him closest—Nature gay and Nature pensive; all her changing moods delighted him. In a charming and sympathetic memoir Duncan Campbell Scott tells how after a long forced rest, when it was almost spring he would love to walk about slowly in the sunshine observing the process of nature—the advent of the warblers and the triumph of the first fruit blossoms. Back to the woods he always came from the troubled cities; back to the cool glades and dim recesses in search of quietude and solace. For earth was to him a soft-cheeked mother, and her voice was his inspiration and his comfort. But after all he has shown himself clearer and revealed his spirit better in his works; his smallest poems are more eloquent biography than the most skilfully prepared appreciation could be. Nothing, for instance, could present a better example of his dream and flower philosophy, his intimate vision and of the man himself than this simple, almost whimsical sonnet which he has called

WINTER-THOUGHT

The wind-swayed daisies, that on every side
   Throng the wide fields in whispering companies,
   Serene and gently smiling like the eyes
Of tender children long beatified,
The delicate thought-wrapped buttercups that glide
   Like sparks of fire above the wavering grass,
   And swing and toss with all the airs that pass,
Yet seem so peaceful, so preoccupied;
These are the emblems of pure pleasures flown,
   I scarce can think of pleasure without these.
Even to dream of them is to disown
   The cold forlorn midwinter reveries,
Lulled with the perfume of old hopes new-blown,
   No longer dreams, but dear realities.

Here is the very refinement of poetic speech; an expression so softened and delicate that the entire fourteen lines suggest a wistful musing rather than any conscious thought. And what exquisite images are here embodied:

Wind-swayed daisies . . .
   Serene and gently smiling like the eyes
Of tender children long beatified,

and the picture of

delicate thought-wrapped buttercups that glide
Like sparks of fire above the wavering grass.

It is through such passages of beauty that the sonnet with all its restrictions and limitations becomes the most ravishing of all the classic forms. And it is in the sonnet that Lampman is at the very height of his genius. In all of his sonnets, and there are over a hundred in the second edition of his collected poems, there is apparently not only a complete mastery of the subtlest technical nuances, but a variety of treatment that makes them all the more remarkable. Not content to reflect the mood of a moment, or paint a passing picture, he has drawn upon all the arts for their individual characteristics. The result is that his sonnets appeal to all the senses—they tremble with sound, they dazzle with color; they are pictures set to music—plastic and pulsing.

Like a long drawn note on a muted violin or a young mother's wonderful sigh is this poignant and searching bit of melody played on a lyre of fourteen strings.

TO THE LUTE-PLAYER

Oh, take the lute this brooding hour for me—
The golden lute, the hollow, crying lute—
Nor even call me with thine eyes; be mute,
And touch the strings; yea, touch them tenderly;
Touch them and dream, till all thine heart in thee
Grow great and passionate and sad and wild.
Then on me, too, as on thine heart, O child,
The marvelous light, the stress divine shall be,
And I shall see, as with enchanted eyes,
The unveiled vision of this world flame by,
Battles and griefs and storms and phantasies,
The gleaming joy, the ever-seething fire,
The hero's triumph and the martyr's cry,
The pain, the madness, the unsearched desire.

If ever a sonnet could be lyric this is the very sublimation of song.

Oh, take the lute this brooding hour for me—
The golden lute, the hollow . . . lute

is like a low refrain in which is blended all the yearning and the weltschmerz that the contemplation of things beautiful always awakens, awakens even more than it lulls. Music, which he felt more intuitively than anything else, was always present, even in his severest moments. Repetitions of phrases and their alternatives, skilful balancing of similar sounding words, and the varied use of accented rhythms tended to give many of his sonnets more actual melody than one usually finds in widely heralded "songs." In "Earth—the Stoic" we discover what is possibly one of the best examples of these melodic turns and echoes in the first few lines:

> Earth, like a goblet empty of delight,
> Empty of summer and balm-breathing hours,
> Empty of music, empty of all flowers.

Thus every word became a separate instrument in his hands; he knew all its tones and overtones, its powers and possibilities. He played lovingly upon it until he had sounded every haunting harmony and melting modulation, until all the subtle and exquisite changes were blended with the other voices in a series of symphonic passages. He would but touch an ordinarily prosaic and unresponsive word, and it became a thing of infinite suggestion, vital with beauty and throbbing with imagination. For purely pictorial effect I know of no sonnet in the English language that excels the following masterpiece. It is more than a picture—it is a painting so perfect that it contains heat and sound and all the faintly stirring life of a summer's day itself.

AMONG THE ORCHARDS

Already in the dew-wrapped vineyards dry
   Dense weights of heat press down. The large bright drops
   Shrink in the leaves. From dark acacia tops
The nuthatch flings his short reiterate cry;
And ever as the sun mounts hot and high
   Thin voices crowd the grass. In soft long strokes
   The wind goes murmuring through the mountain oaks.
Faint wefts creep out along the blue and die.

I hear far in among the motionless trees—
   Shadows that sleep upon the shaven sod—
   The thud of dropping apples. Reach on reach
Stretch plots of perfumed orchard, where the bees
   Murmur among the full-fringed goldenrod
   Or cling half-drunken to the rotting peach.

It is doubtful whether any of our poets could have written these lines except Keats—Keats to whom Lampman was so strangely affiliated. Not only in the love of sensuous sounding words and luxuriant phrases but in their attitude toward life was this similarity striking. Neither of them cared for the companionship of throngs or the clamor of cities; they were happiest if they could be "wrapped round in thought, content to watch and dream." Both of them attempted to hold and reawaken the fleeting sensations of taste and touch by some colorful adjective or a tinted phrase—to renew by mere words the spiritual and esthetic emotions and pleasures which cannot be reproduced. Both were strongly imbued with the lyric spirit, and each of them completed just one play. Lampman, however, never attained the highest peaks of song but for a few golden moments—his singing was never of that sustained and god-like beauty that is the epitome of Keats. But if he lacked this, there was one note he struck more effectively that Keats never possessed. And that was the note of poetic psychology. Not the shadowy and equivocal symbolism that so many of our really able writers affect, nor yet the merely modern "realism" which is the exaggerated vision of a thing that is not even real, but a psychology at one time poetic and searching—so mysterious that it clothes with beauty, so illuminating that it lays bare. Of such an order is this remarkable poem which, by the way, is included with four other selections from Lampman in Stedman's *Victorian Anthology*. It is probably the only widely known and much-quoted of all his works.

A FORECAST

What days await this woman, whose strange feet
Breathe spells, whose presence makes men dream like wine,
  Tall, free and slender as the forest pine;
Whose form is moulded music, through whose sweet
Frank eyes I feel the very heart's least beat,
  Keen, passionate, full of dreams and fire:

How in the end, and to what man's desires
Shall all this yield, whose lips shall these lips meet?
One thing I know: if he be great and pure
This love, this fire, this beauty shall endure;
  Triumph and hope shall lead him by the palm;
But if not this, some differing thing he be
That dream shall break in terror, he shall see
  The whirlwind ripen, where he sowed the calm.

But lest it be thought from these pages that Lampman was
either mute or inglorious in any other but the sonnet form,
let it be understood that several of his ballads such as "The
Violinist," "War," and "The Vase of Ibn Mokbil" are particularly noteworthy; that his "David and Abigail" (which
though a three-act play he has called even more fitly "a
poem in dialogue") contains passages of rich feeling and
noble declamation, and that his purely songful lyrics are
among his best endeavours. "Between the Rapids," "Easter
Eve," "The Song of Pan," and "Before Sleep" are each
of them a perfect expression which no art could better.
The first verse of the last-named is so ethereal that it would
be unfair not to quote it in this connection:

> Now the crouching nets of sleep
>   Stretch about and gather nigh,
> And the midnight dim and deep
>   Like a spirit passes by.
> Trailing from her crystal dress
> Dreams and silent frostiness.

Nor should this recital end without including these brief
but majestic verses "With the Night":

> O doubts, dull passions, and base fears
> That harassed and oppressed the day,
> Ye poor remorses and vain tears,
> That shook this house of clay;
>
> All heaven to the western bars
> Is glittering with the darker dawn;
> Here, with the earth, the night, the stars,
> Ye have no place: begone!

Whether Lampman will ever be one of those whose
names are the pride and envy of the world is answered by
the question itself. Whether he will even achieve the subdued glory of the lesser bards is a doubtful matter. Sometimes one thinks his voice was never meant for earth, but
for "some world far from ours, where music and moonlight
and feeling are one." It seems that a tone so intense and
rapturous must continue to vibrate even after the singer
is mute.

But even if all this ecstasy should perish, if all the lovely
color should fade, and the inspired music be quite forgotten, the spirit beneath them, the divine energy that
wrought these wonders can never die. Whether its reincarnation will be that of a singing bird or a dreaming flower;
a shaft of spring sunlight or even another poet shall blend
all of these, no one will ever know. His soul was as careless
of glorification as he was of earthly fame. He renounced
ambition and his whole life was a splendid resignation.
Voicing his creed he summed up all his aims and aspira-
tions in a humble yet glorious cadence when he sang:

> From other lips let stormy numbers flow,
> By others let great epics be compiled;
> For me, the dreamer, 'tis enough to know
> The lyric words, the fervour sweet and wild.
> I sit me in the windy grass and grow
> As wise as age, as joyous as a child.

ARCHIBALD LAMPMAN

LAWRENCE J. BURPEE

"I can remember," wrote William Dean Howells, "no poem of Archibald Lampman's in which I was not sensible of an atmosphere of exquisite refinement, breathing a scent as rare as if it drifted from beds of arbutus or thickets of eglantine, where he led the way. His pure spirit was electrical in every line; he made no picture of the nature he loved in which he did not supply the spectator with the human interest of his own genial presence, and light up the scene with the lamp of his keen and beautiful intelligence. He listened for its breath, its pulse; he peered into its face, and held his ear to its heart, with a devotion none the less impassioned because his report of what he saw and heard was so far from vehemence or straining. Sometimes in his transport with its loveliness he could not help crowding his verse with the facts that were all so dear to him; but one knew from its affluence that not a scent, or sound, or sight of the Canadian summer was lost upon his quick sense, and one saw how he could not bear to forbid any in a world finding its way through his music into art for the first time. The stir of leaf, of wings, of foot; the drifting odours of wood and field; the colours of flowers, of skies, of dusty roads and shadowy streams and solitary lakes all so preciously new, gave his reader the thrill of the intense life of the northern solstice."

To those who had the privilege of Archibald Lampman's friendship, and knew him as man and poet, this appreciation of Mr. Howells' cannot seem exaggerated. His verse reveals everywhere the qualities that belonged to the man—absolute sincerity, seriousness lightened by glimpses

"Archibald Lampman," by Lawrence J. Burpee. From his *A Little Book of Canadian Essays* (Toronto: Musson, 1909), pp. 30-42. By permission of Musson Book Co.

of delicate humour, and a sympathy so broad that it might not be confined to mankind, but must embrace all Nature, animate and inanimate. He was ever true to his ideals in his poetry as in his life. His verse reflected his own pure, high-minded nature. He was in very truth an ideal poet, clean-hearted, broad-minded, clear-sighted, free from all affectation and conventionality, strong in support of what he held to be the right, but otherwise most modest, unassuming, and self-forgetful. His point of view is so admirably summed up in that one of his sonnets called "Outlook," that one cannot forbear quoting it—although it is probably one of the best known of his poems.

> Not to be conquered by these headlong days,
> But to stand free: to keep the mind at brood
> On life's deep meaning, nature's altitude
> Of loveliness, and time's mysterious ways;
> At every thought and deed to clear the haze
> Out of our eyes, considering only this,
> What man, what life, what love, what beauty is,
> This is to live, and win the final praise.
>
> Though strife, ill fortune, and harsh human need
> Beat down the soul, at moments blind and dumb
> With agony; yet, patience—there shall come
> Many great voices from life's outer sea,
> Hours of strange triumph, and, when few men heed,
> Murmurs and glimpses of eternity.

In reading Lampman's poems, from the very first the sympathetic ear catches cadences of that harmonious music of the wild woods to which he held the key:

> Ah, I have wandered with unwearied feet,
> All the long sweetness of an April day,
> Lulled with cool murmurs and the drowsy beat
> Of partridge wings in secret thickets gray,
> The marriage hymns of all the birds at play,
> The faces of sweet flowers, and easeful dreams
> Beside slow reaches of frog-haunted streams.

In the very last poem he wrote—the sonnet, "Winter Uplands"—when the hand of death was pressing urgently upon his soul, the same sympathetic insight is found, the same keen perception of the jealously guarded secrets of nature, the same absence of strain, egotism, and passion. It is not, perhaps, altogether without significance that while the above verses, some of his earliest, are devoted to Nature's spring-time, his last word was given to midwinter. It was a part of his broad sympathies that he could find beauty and helpfulness in the storm and stress of our northern winter, as well as in the haunting charm of a Canadian mid-summer's day.

In the poem "Heat" is developed one of the most distinctive qualities of Lampman's verse—its almost marvellous picturesqueness and imagery:

> From plains that reel to southward, dim,
>   The road runs by me white and bare;
> Up the steep hill it seems to swim
>   Beyond, and melt into the glare.
>
> Upward, half-way, or it may be
>   Nearer the summit, slowly steals
> A hay-cart, moving dustily
>   With idly clacking wheels.
>
> By his cart's side the wagoner
>   Is slouching slowly at his ease,
> Half hidden in the windless blur
>   Of white dust puffing to his knees.

And in the very next poem, "Among the Timothy," still another characteristic is revealed—his gift for striking phrases, phrases that sparkle like gems, sentences that appeal irresistibly to one's sense of the beautiful, and live in the memory after the rest of the poem has dropped out of sight:

Hither and thither o'er the rocking grass
The little breezes, blithe as they are blind,
Teasing the slender blossoms pass and pass,
Soft-footed children of the gipsy wind,
To taste of every purple-fringed head
Before the bloom is dead;
And scarcely heed the daisies that, endowed
With stems so short they cannot see, upbear
Their innocent sweet eyes distressed, and stare
Like children in a crowd.

Two other qualities that mark Lampman's verse and give it distinction are the jealous care with which it was polished and re-polished before allowed to depart from the workshop of the poet's mind, and his unerring instinct in the choice of words. It follows that one may search in vain throughout his poems for a crude expression, an awkward line, or even a false rhyme or metre. His verse is also instinct with colour and music, and possesses in its highest development that true "lyrical cry" which is one of the attributes of true poetry, and of true poetry alone.

Of the more definitely human studies, perhaps nothing that Lampman wrote is much finer than "Easter Eve." It possesses, in its degree, something of the sombre grandeur of Dante, and reminds one, in its spiritual significance and dramatic power, of Stephen Phillips' "Christ in Hades."

In "The Monk" we have another graphic and sombre picture, though of a different kind. The forlorn hermit is seen in his cell, his lonely cell, trying to read, and brooding over what "might have been":

With every word some torturing dream is born;
And every thought is like a step that scares
Old memories up to make him weep and mourn.
He cannot turn, but from their latchless lairs
The weary shadows of his lost delight
Rise up like dusk-birds through the lonely night.

In the "Child's Music Lesson" is revealed still another phase of the poet's broad personality—his tender love for children; and in such verses as "An Athenian Reverie" he shows his knowledge of the history and literature, and the very atmosphere, of ancient Greece. Here, too, one gets another glimpse of the poet's personal outlook:

> Happy is he,
> Who, as a watcher, stands apart from life,
> From all life and his own, and thus from all,
> Each thought, each deed, and each hour's brief event,
> Draws the full beauty, sucks its meaning dry.

Lampman's friend and biographer, Duncan Campbell Scott, has afforded us some interesting details of the poet's personality and his methods of work:

His poems were principally composed as he walked to and from his ordinary employment in the city, or upon excursions into the country, or as he paced about his writing-room. Lines invented under these conditions would be transferred to manuscript books, and finally, after they had been perfected, would be written out carefully in his clear, strong handwriting in volumes of a permanent kind.

Although this was his favourite and natural method of composing, he frequently wrote his lines as they came to him; and in many of his note-books can be traced the development of poems through the constant working of his fine instinct for form and expression. . . .

To write verses was the one great delight of his life. Everything in his world had reference to poetry. He was restless with a sense of burden when he was not composing, and deep with content when some stanza was taking form gradually in his mind.

He was not a wide reader; books of history and travel were his favourites. During his last illness he read *The Ring and the Book*, the novels of Jane Austen, and continued a constant reading of Greek by a reperusal of Pindar, the *Odyssey*, and the tragedies of Sophocles.

Matthew Arnold was his favourite modern poet, and he read his works oftener than those of any other; but Keats was the only poet whose method he carefully studied.

Perhaps one of the most entirely satisfactory poems he wrote was the sonnet-sequence, "The Largest Life," written toward the close of his short life, and beginning:

> I lie upon my bed and hear and see,
> The moon is rising through the glistening trees:
> And momently a great and sombre breeze,
> With a vast voice returning fitfully,
> Comes like a deep-toned grief. . . .

The last of the three sonnets embodies the sum-total of the poet's gospel—that gospel to which he was faithful to the end:

> There is a beauty at the goal of life,
>   A beauty growing since the world began,
> Through every age and race, through lapse and strife,
>   Till the great human soul completes her span.
> Beneath the waves of storm that lash and burn,
>   The currents of blind passion that appal,
> To listen and keep watch till we discern
>   The tide of sovereign truth that guides it all;
> So to address our spirits to the height,
>   And so attune them to the valiant whole,
> That the great light be clearer for our light,
>   And the great soul the stronger for our soul:
> To have done this is to have lived, though fame
> Remember us with no familiar name.

This was indeed the life that Archibald Lampman led, and, having done so, it matters little enough whether or no fate remembers him with a "familiar name."

ARCHIBALD LAMPMAN

Archibald Lampman was one of the group of young
Canadian poets born while the idea of a federated British
North America was germinating in the minds of Canadians. Thus he escaped the incipient stage of Canada's
colonial days and was born after the period of its literary
crudities. For the majority of writers born at this epoch
were essentially men of native university training. They
were heirs to the worlds of the European poets' creation.
All of them, too, were highly coloured mentally by a study
of the English poets of beauty, who, since the appearance
of Coleridge's magical poems, have handed on the light of
Art like the Athenians of old in their torch race. And
Lampman himself is no exception to the rule. Indeed he
was so overpowered by the influence of one English poet—
Keats—that, in his humble homage to the subtle priest of
Sufism, he has frequently essayed, as I shall endeavour to
show, a mode of expression at once alien and hurtful to his
own bent.

Son of the Anglican Rector of Morpeth, Lampman was
born on November 17th, 1861. He came of German and
Dutch descent and this should not be forgotten, for it accounts in no small degree for that meticulous minuteness
of detail in much of his verse, for its calm nonchalance and
unruffled flow of thought.

He was something of a delicate valetudinarian all his life,
for, when quite a child, he was afflicted by a severe attack
of rheumatic fever from the effects of which he never really
rid himself. Indeed, there is a note of this lingering about
all his verse. He had the delight of a sick man in nature

"Archibald Lampman," by Bernard Muddiman. In *Queen's Quarterly*
22 (January 1915), 233-43.

and healthy things, in the splendid beauty of long summer days. He had, too, a sensibility for bright colour and choice form, which is not seldom attendant on such states of health. But he had not that hectic, feverish sensuousness that marked the outlook of Keats, whom he mistakenly took for his model. Rather his is a sombre, Teutonic mind rapt in a continual *meditatio mortis* in all his best work, not so much expressed, but to the attentive listener always overheard. Again it is never work of a vociferous, animally robust personality—it is too wistful, too tender for that.

He was sent to Trinity College school at Port Hope, Ontario, one of those big private boarding schools, which are run on English Public School lines by English masters. The leading feature of such an early education was a careful drilling in Latin and Greek grammar; for the active side of athletics was rather discountenanced as far as young Lampman was concerned, owing to his precarious health. From this atmosphere, wherein only the really robust benefit, he came to Toronto as a student at Trinity College, as one who had been through the rougher usage of a boarding school. Indeed, at Toronto, the name of Lampman gathered to itself something of the reputation of riotousness so dear to the heart of every undergraduate. As a matter of fact it was simply his poetic temperament trying to express itself; and, since he had come from the rough ways of a boarding school, it naturally, for a time, revealed itself crudely. This in the case of a French boy, for example, would have been impossible. He was, however, recognized at college as a brilliant youth, winning his way through by means of scholarships, which were very necessary, for misfortune and poverty had already overtaken his family.

At college he began to write, but, like many poets, his first efforts were in prose. As a result of his labours one or two chapters of a novel, he afterwards discarded, were written. But prose was not his métier. It was merely a training for his verse work; while his academic reading in Latin and Greek was to help to give his verse that polish so rarely found in Canadian works. But, unfortunately, Latin and Greek are not nearly such valuable assets as the fruits of a technical education. Consequently on leaving college, like so many others, he drifted into teaching, the most heart-breaking and soul-dissecting occupation an artist could find. His assistant mastership at Orangeville High School happily did not last long: for, in 1883, through friendly influence, he obtained a clerkship in the Post Office Department of the Dominion Government at Ottawa. It was a haven of refuge into which far from the busy world's clamour this dreamer was glad to creep, content with the poor pay, because of the short daily task.

Nothing further was to trouble him all his life except poetry. His happy marriage in 1887 and his election in 1895 to the Royal Society of Canada were merely incidents tending to consolidate his poetic enthralment. In actual biography there is nothing else to relate, for in the Post Office Department he remained until he died on February 8th, 1899,[1] without any further wanderings save those of the spirit. However, if life did not give him much scope for new sensations, his intellect was always adventuring. He ordered his days in accordance with his expressed wish:

Oh for a life of leisure and broad hours,
    To think and dream, to put away small things,
    This world's perpetual leaguer of dull naughts;
To wander like the bee among the flowers
    Till old age find us weary, feet and wings
    Grown heavy with the gold of many thoughts.

He delighted to read his classics in peace:

    To till the old world's wisdom till it grew
    A garden for the wandering of our feet.

And in the same way we can picture him through the passionately hot days of summer that bake and burn the countryside round Ottawa, a leisurely wanderer up the charming Welsh scenery of the Gatineau valley or down

---

[1]Lampman died in the early morning of February 10, 1899.

the Ottawa River or among the Rideau Lakes. It was not for him to venture further afield to the bush, much though in spirit he may have longed for it.

A year after he entered the Civil Service, Lampman mailed to Charles G. D. Roberts, then editor of *The Week*, a literary periodical, in Toronto, two poems, which the editor with excellent discrimination accepted. Hence forward Lampman continued to send his poems at intervals to periodicals, particularly those of the better American type like Scribner's, where they received a sympathetic welcome. Other publication for the time he was unable to attain through lack of funds until 1888, when his wife received a legacy, which was generously spent in issuing locally his first little volume, *Among the Millet*.

This volume has a freshness and sweetness his rather limited muse never again attained. He never even maintained the same level. It contains, perhaps, his best work and there is the dew of the dawn on it. And as we leaf its pages "The Frogs," "Heat," "Among the Timothy," "Midnight" and "Between the Rapids" stand out beyond the others. Some of its longer poems, perhaps, are the least satisfactory. For instance, they are mostly exercises in imitation, like that unsuccessful narrative "The Monk," palpably modeled on Keats' well known "Eve of St. Agnes."

In the circumscribed ground of the sonnet Lampman is peculiarly happy in his very first efforts. His minute method of piling up details makes them exquisite medallions of song. In this mode "The Frogs" is composed of five sonnets, each like the perfectly carved bead of a rosary:

I

Breathers of wisdom won without a quest,
   Quaint uncouth dreamers, voices high and strange;
   Flautists of lands where beauty hath no change,
And wintry grief is a forgotten guest,

Sweet murmurers of everlasting rest,
　For whom glad days have ever yet to run,
　And moments are as aeons, and the sun
But ever sunken half-way toward the west.

Often to me who heard you in your day,
　With close rapt ears, it could not choose but seem
The earth, our mother, searching in what way
　Men's hearts might know her spirit's inmost dream;
　Ever at rest beneath life's change and stir,
　Made you her soul, and bade you pipe to her . . .

III

All the day long, wherever pools might be,
　Among the golden meadows, where the air
　Stood in a dream, as it were moored there
For ever in a noon-tide reverie,
Or where the birds made riot of their glee
　In the still woods, and the hot sun shone down,
　Crossed with warm lucent shadows on the brown
Leaf-paven pools, that bubbled dreamily.

Or far away in whispering river meads
　And watery marshes where the brooding noon,
　Full with the wonder of its own sweet boon,
Nestled and slept among the noiseless reeds,
Ye sat and murmured, motionless as they,
　With eyes that dreamed beyond the night and day.

These Shakespearean sonnets may not be packed with
the sad thoughts of a Pascal or the plangent utterances of a
Lucretius, but seldom has this form been handled with
greater musical dexterity. The exactness, too, of the natural
imagery is astonishing. Lampman was one of those naturally endowed with "the lust of the eye." This lends often to
his best verse a vivid richness in its vignettes of the natural
world. Town-bred he has a hunger for nature, a passion for
the soil. As in life he loved to get in the woods and leave
behind the fever and fret of petty official life in the mediocre atmosphere of a village capital; so, in his verse, he
loves to write of the blue bird peeping from the gnarled

thorn, of the vesper sparrows at the forest hem, of the purple-bossed orange cone-flowers. He thought he saw in nature the eternal anodyne for every carking care. Take his poem "Among the Timothy." It is an excellent example of this belief of his in the restoring faculty of nature. He tasted nature as an epicure tastes a bonne-bouche. With what joy he smelt the keen perfume of the ripening grass and feasted on summer sounds. The shrill piping hylas, the warbling vireos, the crazy fiddling of the crickets and the creaking of frogs on the woodland pools—all touched some respondent chord in his own nature. He delights in the snowy trilliums or the rosy tops of fleabane veiled with dew, the fields black with the mould and brown with the loam. Sometimes he comes away with an impression of a landscape such as "a vapour of azure distilled on the opaline green of the fields." The whole movement of the seasons from the bleak Ontario spring through the arid passion of its summer, the gorgeous pageant of the Fall, to the long white winter evokes his salutation. He is the poet of Ontario. In the soundless woods of winter, where the wind alone makes secret stir, he wanders drawing his thoughts closer around him like a cloak ensnared by the very austerity of the beauty of this crystalline world. Secret as the ice-sheeted, snow-hid streams he plods on, a veritable John O'Dreams. June, September, April or mid-winter he has celebrated them all. He has dozens of little vignettes of this pageant of nature, but his best, it seems to me, are those of winter:

> Down the frozen street to market
>   Come the woodmen team by team,
> Squeaking runners, jolting cordwood,
>   Frost-fringed horses jetting steam.
>
> . . . .
>
> Where the frosted creamy splendour
>   Of the morning slants and shines
> On smooth fields and sheeted rivers,
>   Stretching to the western pines.

Something of that solemn melancholy wail that pierces through every phrase of the Russian poets, the voice of the silent whiteness of the snow-clad steppes of the north moans a little in all Lampman's winter pieces. The ancient runic call of ice and snow beneath a pallid moon and silver stars croons wistfully as he recalls:

> The spaces of a white and wintry land
> Swept with the fire of sunset . . .

The beauty of silence, the vastness of dreams, the pessimism of human hopes wails forth half-expressed as he broods on the sad, still wastes of the frozen world.

Perhaps "Between the Rapids" has a far more human interest than the majority of these yards of natural description. It has the romantic charm of Canada's heroic age. Yet it is modern in its setting, that is to say, it is as old and as modern as God's hills and rivers and man's elemental emotions. It is the song of a home-sick voyageur, a French Canadian lumberjack, if you like, paddling past his native village on the river "between the rapids in the evening dusk." Full of melancholy recollection he hears the familiar "loitering bells, the lowing of the cows." He remembers old friends, black-eyed Jeanne whose tongue was never still, wrinkled old Picard, pale Lisette and all the other homely hearts that never cared to range. He wonders, vaguely, if the same lips still repeat the same old shouts. But nothing can hold him by any sacred bond of kith and kin, of love or regret, for he is born wanderer as restless as the river that bears him on.

I have already referred to the longer poems in this volume as exercises of a youthful poet in imitation. There is one particular aspect of this that it would be as well to deal with at once. Keats wrote "Endymion" and other pieces of pretty paganism according to Wordsworth. Lampman, like many a later poet who has read Theocritus and Euripides in his boyhood, has also turned more than once to the dead

classic past in the manner of Keats. But his Hellenic poems
are no more Hellenic in their passion than the memories
of any average lad who has wasted (if you like) hours with a
grammar and Liddell & Scott.[1] Keats, who knew nothing of
Greek paradigms, was a born Greek like Pierre Louys today. Lampman, on the other hand, was no more imbued
with the Hellenic spirit than he was with the Red Indian.
Consequently his "Athenian Reverie," for example, is
really nothing more than a "Lampman Reverie," and is
totally devoid of the Pagan heart's emotions. In other
words, it is Lampman in a pose and is remarkable only for
a certain academic tediousness. For Lampman had the
questioning aspiration of the modern undulant mind of
the Matthew Arnold type. Greek blitheness, Hellenic
gaiety, Athenian irresponsibility and subtlety never evince
themselves in his work any more than a sense of humour.
"Keats was the only poet whose method," says Mr. D. C.
Scott, "he carefully studied." That may be so but he was
not of the company of Keats. If I had to describe him in
this odious comparative method I should hail him as a
child of the Wordsworth school. True, he loves colour and
perfumed words, where Wordsworth used simple, mun-
dane speech; but that was because literary tinsel attracted
him. His feeling for nature, for high thinking and simple
living was Wordsworthian. The Sufistic[2] paradise in which
Keats moved was unknown to this singer of simplicities.
He was not obsessed by the passionate thrills, the spinal
sensualities of Keats. He had little akin to the spirit that
sighed out sonnets, that longed to die a death of luxury.
He had no universality of sensuousness. Lampman's only
sensuousness was in words, not in ideas or feelings. He
might wallow in "Spenserian vowels that elope with ease,"
but born in respectable Ontario he could not swoon

[1] Henry George Liddell and Robert Scott, co-authors of the Greek-
English Lexicon.
[2] Deriving from the pantheism of a mystical sect of Mohammedan
ascetics.

drunken from pleasure's nipple. Nature and books—these alone made up his life. In Ottawa he had small chance for other intellectual life or acquaintance with the arts. Far from artistic movements, the theatres, ballets, cafés, studios, the charm of salons, where women are not only decorative but intellectual centres; many miles away from the world's capitals where fashion and taste are made—the only wonder is, perhaps, that the poet achieved so much. Strange women, strange thoughts like strange drinks were not his earthly portion.

As Masson says, Keats' odes are literally lyrics of sensuous embodiments of the feelings of ennui, fatigue, physical languor and the like, tissued in circumstances and sensation that Lampman never experienced. The intellectual power of Keats is of another order and that order is the hectic. If we wish to find a real reincarnation of Keats we must go to Ernest Dowson or better still to Albert Samain. Lampman confronted with real Keatsian ideas would have felt like a Sunday school in the Moulin Rouge in its maddest nights of old.

Again as to Lampman's hellenic proclivities I can find no more evidence than that you can find in favour of any man who once schoolboywise made out Euripidean choruses and since then has had the disadvantage of being, as Jeffreys said, on occasion mythological. Certainly he is not Greek in his treatment of nature. For as Arthur Stringer aptly said, "he sees nature in a simple light." The Greeks clothed the forces of nature with beautiful forms. Nor again has he the Greek sense of form, which often fairly oozes out of Keats' brain. If you want the Greek spirit in modern literature you must go to the "Mimes" of Marcel Schwob, to "Les Chansons de Bilitis" of Pierre Louys.

Eight years after the appearance of its predecessor, *Lyrics of Earth* appeared at Boston. This volume contains, perhaps, nothing so good as the best of the first book. In fact it is rather a repetition of his former note than something new. And the note now is less liquid, less free. It has not gained in depth or range of rapture. Long poems on the months follow each other. We are treated to long descriptions, but the etching is less firm and the stroke often falters. We are told again to take comfort in the fields and feast on summer sounds. Drink of nature's restful cup and ye shall be filled and ye shall understand. An excellent philosophy, no doubt, but hardly universally satisfying. It has its limitations that soon become as apparent as the limitations of the poet's muse. Neither is it a philosophy of energy or aggression. It is rather impregnated with the humiliation of inertia, of a dreamer wandering in fields that are deaf and dumb to his alien sorrows.

Here again in this second slim volume Lampman is happiest when painting the countryside around Ottawa. "At the Ferry," for example, is a wonderfully accurate impression of the Ottawa river. But pictures, however photographically realistic of nature, are not enough to fascinate. Of course, those humans who are, indeed, favourites of Pan, may spend all their lives in rapt contemplation of the manifold manifestations of nature's wonders; but, page after page of unrelieved description of the "Bird and the Hour," of "After Rain," of "Cloudbreak" is not fulfilling the rich promise offered in *Among the Millet*. In fact a feeling begins to pervade the reader's consciousness that Lampman, after all, said all he had to say amply and sufficiently in his first volume. On that his reputation with one or two exceptions will rest. He had delivered what the Muses had told him and he was now but feebly improvising on the same themes with the best half of his inspiration dissipated. That high attitude of mind, burning with a hard gem-like flame, Pater speaks of somewhere, and which sees all the magic pageantry of every minute from the cloudflake to the flower cannot be continually maintained. Indeed, Lampman has lost some of it himself in vain reiteration and we are filled with doubts as his inspiration visibly fails.

At the time of his death in 1899, a third volume *Alcyone*

was in the press. It is far more bookish than its predecessors. The lover of the fields has gone more now to his study for inspiration than in his youth. The only really happy land, after all, is the land of dreams. The comfort of the meadows of dreams has grown more potent than the fields of the natural world. His Cockaigne now is no longer the nearest copse but the land of Pallas, where a man can take this sorry scheme of things we call the world and shatter it and rebuild it after his desire.

His nature poems have become more than ever exercises in description. They have become also wearisome. We first sigh, then yawn, in reading them. The volume falls from our hands and we are asleep. His vein of ideas has run out. He is simply reworking the same old vein and the gold is far to seek and hard to find. He has, in fact, expressed all he had to say. Death has robbed us of nothing in his early demise.[1] His best songs were his first. What cold pieces of rhetoric, for example, are "Chione" and "Vivia Perpetua." "The City of the End of Things" is Lampman's "lost in a tangle of description."[2] The earnestness of the poet cannot now make up for his limited ideas and limited vocabulary. The persuasive freshness of the first volume is gone. As I leaf this volume I am reminded of fruit that once dew-kissed, juicy and roseate glistened amid green foliage, but has now grown dull and tasteless through prolonged exposure in a greengrocer's window.

In 1900 a collected edition of his works was edited by friends and Mr. Scott, who as a civil servant had known his colleague for the greater part of his life, wrote an introduction to the volume. This is the most valuable addition to our knowledge, for otherwise the edition gives us no new verse of any value and is indeed overbulky with verse too jealously preserved. His friend's sympathetic study, however, must be hailed as lucid and as healthy a note on

[1] "A Glance at Lampman," by A. Y. Stringer, *Can. Mag.*, April, 1894.
[2] "Canadian Poetry," by Gordon Waldron, *Can. Mag.*, December, 1896.

a comrade as has ever prefaced a departed Canadian poet's work. It is admirable and contains none of the senseless gush that the advertising spirit of the new world has grafted into its literary notices. It narrates simply the incidents of the poet's life and personality. Criticism, laudation and condonation are alike banished from its excellent periods and as we read an image of this delicate young poet rises before us. "His poems were principally composed as he walked to and from his ordinary employment in the city, or upon excursions into the country, or as he paced about his writing room. . . . To write verses was the one great delight of his life. Everything in his world has reference to poetry. He was restless with a sense of burden when he was not composing, and deep with content when some stanza was taking form gradually in his mind."

There are two ways of being a poet, says a dreamer in Jean Richepin's "Madame André"—as a fakir or a Roman Emperor. If you are Nero, Heliogabalus, you live poetry. You have your epopees of power, your odes of voluptuousness. You are lyrism in flower. If not, you must dream of what you have not. And Lampman was essentially a dreamer of dreams. Had he been a more feverish dreamer he might have written greater poems. He would have handled the hair of comets and Venus would have called him by the names of birds. As a matter of fact, however, his were mild dreams, meditative, attuned to a love of placid days and ways. The atmosphere of a government office is not exciting oxygen for a poet. If, however, it had been a bureau in Paris instead of a small village capital, he might have written—well, it is useless to say what. As it is he has given us a handful of perfect sonnets and one or two poems, which should be bound together in a new volume to stand for Lampman in Canadian literature, while the bulk of his collected volume can easily be dispensed with. Lampman himself staked his reputation on his "Sonnets" and in this he was right. The peculiarly

limited field of this form of verse was best suited for his
mental strength. A solitary thought could be adorned in
all its becoming glory. The slow movement of the surgent
and resurgent wave of the sonnet kept admirable pace
with the gait of his brain. For he had no wide perceptions
of experience in the splendid wayfaring of life. His existence had always been sedentary and sheltered, the busy
marts of big cities, the dramatic possibilities of great
pasisons, the melodies that men play on women's bodies
had passed him by. Poetry like a narcotic had drugged
him and left him on an enchanted isle away from the
world of action—a spellbound minstrel of song—the Canadian poets' poet.

THE POETRY OF ARCHIBALD LAMPMAN

G. H. UNWIN

The year 1880, which saw the publication of *Orion and
Other Poems,* marked the beginning of a new era in our
literature. Dr. J. D. Logan first drew attention to this and
welcomed the appearance of Mr. Roberts' volume as the
first fruit of the "Canadian Renaissance." Within the next
twenty years a number of our best known poets emerged
in print; these included the following names—a goodly list:
Roberts, Lampman, Campbell, Carman, Isabella Crawford, the two Scotts, Drummond, Pauline Johnson. Curiously enough, all, with the exception of Miss Crawford and
Dr. Drummond, were born between 1860 and 1862. So

"The Poetry of Archibald Lampman," by G. H. Unwin. In *University
Magazine* 16 (February 1917), 55-73.

that these three years have a peculiar significance as marking the birth of a group of poets certainly the most important in the history of Canadian verse. Some of these have achieved popularity in their own country, all have acquired literary standing in other countries, and have contributed work which constitutes a permanent addition to our literature.

Of purely lyric poets the most popular in the group is Archibald Lampman. There have been four editions of his complete poems published within the space of ten years (1905-1915); which in itself is a testimonial to the poet's charm and a proof that the Canadian reading public is not so undiscriminating as some would have us believe. It is not reasonable to expect that the nature poems of Lampman should be so widely read as "The Cremation of Sam McGee" and poems of that species. Service has stormed the citadel of public favour and has now achieved the supreme honour of being filmed for the "movies"! Less than a week ago I saw the following poster:

THURSDAY AND FRIDAY
THE POEM CLASSIC
THE SHOOTING OF DAN MCGREW
BY
ROBERT W. SERVICE

However, no mere lyrist could hope to achieve the popularity of him who created "The Lady That's Known As Lou." The fact that the publishers in producing the fourth edition of Lampman's poems are still obeying "numerous and earnest requests" proves that there is a considerable proportion of readers who do not confine their attentions to the vaudeville school of poets.

This is distinctly cheering. It shows that literary appreciation is developing together with, or perhaps in spite of, the business spirit. Professor Cappon says that the modern public seems to require a vigorous presentation of life before listening to any ideal or imaginative strain from a poet. This would account for the well-merited popularity of Dr. Drumond's charming Habitant poems, and also for the work of Robert Service, which in spite of crudeness and frequent melodrama is always vigorous. It cannot, however, explain the vogue of Lampman's nature verse, lyrical, contemplative, essentially the poetry of meditation rather than of life and movement. The question arises then: how does Lampman succeed where others equally gifted have apparently failed? In what particular qualities are we to find the secret of his appeal? If this question can be answered satisfactorily, we are on the road to producing useful criticism. It is a great pity that Professor James Cappon, who has written so illuminating an estimate of poetry of Captain C. G. D. Roberts, has not thought fit to pass public judgment on other Canadian poets. A few more articles like "Roberts and the Influence of his Times," which apeared in the twenty-fourth volume of the *Canadian Magazine*, would do much to clear the way for succeeding poets and educate public taste.

I. *Among the Millet*

The first volume of Lampman's poems *Among the Millet*, was published at the author's risk in 1888. The title, though suggestive, is perhaps unfortunate. Millet is not a characteristic Canadian crop, being generally grown under exceptional circumstances such as a particularly wet season or as a catch crop. However, this is a technicality which perhaps has little to do with the subject in hand. The first twenty poems are pure nature worship in a form very characteristic of the writer; long descriptive poems, landscapes in verse. Many of these, in structure and phrasing, are often strongly reminiscent of Keats. Like Roberts, Lampman modelled his verse more on the method of Keats than of any other; but he did not possess—perhaps fortunately for himself—his brother poet's power of adopting the exact tone and style of another, while producing an original thought. As Professor Cappon points out, this fatal facility of Roberts lends to much of his work the impression of poetical experiment. The whole of Lampman's work, on the other hand, bears the impress of his own personality. Though it is easy to trace in his verse the influence of Keats' style and Arnold's thought, and though at times we catch echoes of Wordsworth and Tennyson, he is not in any sense an eclectic poet. A native genius, moulded and ripened by a study of the masters of English verse, but distinctly fresh and Canadian. The first volume is thoroughly representative of Lampman's finished thought and style, and such poems as "April," "The Frogs," "Heat," "Among the Timothy," are probably equal to anything he produced subsequently. Here is his characteristic wealth of detail joined with selective power: the phrasing is musical, the pictures vivid and there is always that touch of realism which gives him what the critics call "substance." The following passage from "Among the Timothy" is one out of many examples:

> From the green grass the small grasshoppers' din
> Spreads soft and silvery thin,
> And ever and anon a murmur steals
> Into mine ears of toil that moves alway,
> The crackling rustle of the pitchforked hay
> And lazy jerk of wheels.

From the same poem come the following lines, to which possibly some literary puritans might object, as being fanciful or overstrained. The point about this passage, however, is that it is a very "heightened and telling way" of describing the wind in the poplar. It brings the thrill of recognition.

Not far to fieldward in the central heat,
Shadowing the clover, a pale poplar stands
With glimmering leaves that when the wind comes, beat
Together like innumerable small hands,
And with the calm, as in vague dreams astray,
Hang wan and silver grey.

About some of these poems there is a Wordsworthian
atmosphere of serious reflection, and the blank verse of
"Winter Hues Recalled" reminds one of parts of the
"Excursion." The point of view, however, is not that of
Wordsworth. Lampman's attitude toward Nature is primarily aesthetic; the beauty of the scene holds him in
thrall, but the "still, sad music of humanity" rings but
faintly in his ears. The calm strength of external nature
affords relief from the fever of modern life; and from this
source he draws courage and faith to live rightly. There is,
however, no attempt to establish a definite philosophy of
life. The poet, wisely perhaps, steers clear of that whirl-
pool. To illustrate Lampman's usual mental attitude to
nature and humanity I shall quote three stanzas from
"Freedom."

> Over the swamps with their pensive noises
> Where the burnished cup of the marigold gleams,
> Skirting the reeds, where the quick winds shiver
> On the swelling breast of the dimpled river,
> And the blue of the kingfisher hangs and poises,
> Watching a spot by the edge of the stream.
>
> Up to the hills where our tired hearts rest,
> Loosen, and halt and regather their dreams;
> Up to the hills where the winds restore us
> Clearing our eyes to the beauty before us,
> Earth with the glory of life on her breast,
> Earth with the gleam of her cities and streams.
>
> Here we shall commune with her and no other,
> Care and the battle of life shall cease;
> Men, her degenerate children, behind us,
> Only the might of her beauty shall bind us,
> Full of rest as we gaze on the face of our mother,
> Earth in the health and the strength of her peace.

In this volume also are several narrative poems of a
romantic strain, among which may be mentioned especially, "The King's Handmaiden," "Abu Midjan," "The

Organist," "The Monk." The last of these is the most ambitious, a stanzaic poem of some three hundred lines, describing the persecution of a pair of lovers, Nino and Leonora, and their final escape. The scene is laid in Pisa, apparently at the period when the Florentine tyrants were crushing that unfortunate city in their grip; that is to say, in the first half of the 15th century. Reference is made to Messer Gianni, the tyrant, to whom Leonora is forcibly affianced by a mercenary father. Leonora escapes in the dress of a monk and visits her lover, Nino, bearing a goblet of poisoned wine. Without revealing herself she tells the story of her own persecution, but pretends that Leonora has destroyed herself, and has sent the monk as a messenger to her lover, bidding him drink the poisoned wine and join her in Heaven. Nino's constancy is equal to the test; he raises the goblet to his lips, when the supposed monk dashes it to the ground and stands revealed as his mistress. They then escape to a "kindlier shore." As an illustration of the style, I quote one stanza:

> She dashes from her brow the pented hood;
> The dusky robe falls rustling to her feet;
> And there she stands as aye in dreams she stood.
> Ah, Nino, see! Sure man did never meet
> So warm a flower from such a sombre bud,
> So trembling fair, so wan, so pallid sweet.
> Aye, Nino, down like saint upon thy knee,
> And soothe her hands with kisses warm and free.

It is obvious that in this poem the method of Keats has been carefully studied; but having admitted this much we have said about all there is to say. The most unreasoning admirer would hesitate to compare it with "The Eve of St. Agnes." Popular approval has fastened itself upon Lampman's nature verse and has, perhaps justly, ignored his attempts to reproduce classical and romantic themes. This is due partly to the temperament of the writer himself and partly to the spirit of the age in which he lived. The leisurely meditative quality of Lampman's verse did not supply the action and movement necessary to the telling of a story. One has only to read a few pages of the last poem in the volume, "The Story of an Affinity," to realize that in the long narrative poem he was completely out of his element. Then, again, modern life seems to be too full and varied to permit any great interest in classical or mediaeval themes. Roberts' earlier volumes, *Orion* and *Actaeon,* are of this type, and, as a consequence, are known only to critics and students; and Roberts has a wider scholarship, a more vigorous touch and a far greater facility in this kind of poetry than Lampman possessed.

The volume concludes with a number of sonnets mainly reflective in character, among them some of the best known and most popular; "Outlook," "Aspiration," "Knowledge," "The City," might almost be said to have become common property. Lampman said of his own sonnets: "Here, after all, is my best work." His judgment upon himself was severely critical, and Mr. Duncan Campbell Scott, in his excellent memoir, tells us that he was never satisfied. He had the restless ambition of the conscientious artist, as expressed in Tennyson's "Ulysses":

> Yet all experience is an arch wherethro'
> Gleams that untravell'd world, whose margin fades
> For ever and for ever, when I move.

Lampman evidently took his art most seriously and lavished his whole strength upon it. The accusation of careless, off-hand composition, which has so frequently been made against Canadian poets, has no bearing here. Indeed his diligent attention to choice of phrase and metrical arrangement has laid him open to the charge of occasional laboriousness, particularly in some of the longer poems. The sonnet, however, by its compactness, disciplines a mind which carries a wealth of detail. It enforces a mental pruning, leaving only the choicest fruit. Many of Lampman's sonnets are masterpieces of construction and

phrasing, striking the happy mean between the severe and
the ornamental style, with just enough of the poet's own
thoughts to give them a personal value to the reader.
Selection among them is difficult, but I will quote one of
the more purely descriptive type, a triumph of keen
observation and beautiful phrasing:

> How still it is here in the woods. The trees
> Stand motionless as if they did not dare
> To stir, lest it should break the spell. The air
> Hangs quiet as spaces in a marble frieze.
> Even this little brook that runs at ease,
> Whispering and gurgling in its knotted bed,
> Seems but to deepen, with its curling thread
> Of sound, the shadowy sun-pierced silences.
> Sometimes a hawk screams, or a woodpecker
> Startles the stillness from its fixed mood
> With his loud careless tap. Sometimes I hear
> The dreamy whitethroat from some far-off tree
> Pipe slowly on the listening solitude,
> His five pure notes succeeding pensively.

II. *Lyrics of Earth*

The next volume, *Lyrics of Earth*, might be described
as a picture gallery of the seasons. The poems are arranged
in a kind of general sequence following the seasonal
changes. The longer poems, "The Meadow," "June,"
"Comfort of the Fields," "September," "An Autumn Landscape," have a fullness of detail which appeals primarily
to the nature student. "Lyrics of Earth" may be said to
perform the same service for Ontario as Roberts' volume,
Songs of the Common Day, has done for the Maritime
Provinces, and especially New Brunswick. Taken as a
whole the poet's touch is lighter than in the first volume,
the verse more varied, lines and stanzas shorter. There is
an infectious lilt to the movement of these verses taken
from the lyric "In May."

> The sowers in the furrows go;
> The lusty river brimmeth on;
> The curtains from the hills are gone;
> The leaves are out; and lo,
>
> The silvery distance of the day,
> The light horizons, and between
> The glory of the perfect green,
> The tumult of the May.

We pass through a succession of bright pictures of various seasons, all of which show Lampman's characteristic treatment of landscape. First an extraordinarily close observation, which, however, never obscures the broad impression but always preserves the keynote of nature's mood; second, a faculty of happy phrase which endows even commonplace or unnoticed details with interest and beauty. It is this ability to see and show beauty where it is not always recognized which constitutes much of his charm for the ordinary reader. Here is a realistic description of a scene on the Ottawa:

> A tug-boat up the farther shore
> Half pants, half whistles in her draught,
> The cadence of a creaking oar
> Falls drowsily; a corded raft
> Creeps slowly in the noon-day gleam,
> And wheresoe'er a shadow creeps
> The men lie by, or half adream,
> Stand leaning at the idle sweeps.

The features individually taken are prosaic enough; no doubt many a poet would have left them out of the scene, particularly the snorting tug-boat. But this is not the way of Lampman, with whom truth in description is vital. This independence is amply repaid by the sense of reality of which the reader, even when the poet is in the most exalted and imaginative moods, is always conscious. In the passage quoted above the mental picture is vivid and compact, and

the whole is redeemed from the prosaic by a light touch
or phrase here and there, a spot of colour on a subdued
background.

A characteristic feature of the woodland scenes is the
constant reference to birds. Here again the accuracy of the
poet's methods becomes evident. There is, it is true, a kind
of individual characterization which is not altogether
scientific; but Lampman never trades on poetic license.
His descriptions are true, both scientifically and psycho-
logically. In simpler words his imagination, while active,
never runs away from actual facts. One feels that the man
who is talking really knows something about birds: he not
only describes their colours and notes but sketches their
characters with sure, deft touches. Here is an example
from "The Meadow":

> The bluebird, peeping from the gnarled thorn,
> Prattles upon his frolic flute, or flings,
> In bounding flight across the golden morn,
> An azure gleam from off his splendid wings.
> Here the slim-pinioned swallows sweep and pass
> Down to the far-off river; the black crow
> With wise and wary visage to and fro
> Settles and stalks about the withered grass.

There is no lack of examples: the song sparrow, "first
preacher in the naked wilderness," the bob-o-link, "with
tinkle of glassy bells," the vaulting high-ho, the lusty
robin, the genial if discordant blackbird, the solitary
thrush as he "tunes magically his music of fine dreams,"
the snow-birds, "like flurries of wind-driven snow," and
many others. These dainty figures move continually across
the stage, an airy chorus to the drama of Nature.

III. *Alcyone*—SONNETS

In the third volume, *Alcyone,* which did not leave the
publisher's hands till after Lampman's death, the proportion of purely descriptive poems is smaller; the volume

contains more of the author's personal reflections on human life. This change is a natural development, to be observed in any of our Canadian poets who have produced continuous work. The evolution in mental attitude is very clearly marked in the case of C. G. D. Roberts, and can be realized by comparing practically any poem, taken at random from *Orion,* with *Songs of the Common Day,* and these in turn with *The Book of the Native.* Here the poet passes from the romantic style to impressionistic nature verse, and thence to a more reflective, semiphilosophical nature poetry. The same change is to be found in the verse of Mr. Wilfred Campbell when we pass from the *Lake Lyrics* to that collection of poems entitled *Elemental and Human Verse.* Mr. Campbell insists strongly upon the human application, often so strongly as to injure the artistic effect. With Lampman, on the other hand, there is no definite division between the purely descriptive and the reflective, though the third volume contains a larger proportion of poems with a moral application than do the earlier ones. There is, however, no trace of didactic utterance; neither Roberts nor Lampman expresses himself with that emphasis which characterizes the work of their great contemporary, Campbell. A moral truth is suggested, not asserted; there is little attempt at argument. Those readers must go elsewhere, who like poetry which expounds theories and transforms itself into a vehicle of philosophic discussion.

The star, "Alcyone," represents the height of human aspiration, remote, never attainable, but ever present and ever burning. It is the Gleam of Merline, varying in brightness and shade, but always compelling man to follow knowledge, and strive after the highest. In the first poem, from which the volume takes its name, the vague desire of aspiring humanity is given utterance:

> For what is life to thee,
> Turning toward the primal light,
> With that stern and silent face,

> If thou canst not be
> Something radiant and august as night,
> Something wide as space?

Lampman's whole-souled devotion to the highest view of art and its function is reflected in all his work, which has the seriousness that Matthew Arnold considered indispensable to the best poetry. His philosophy may be nebulous, incomplete, but what true poet was ever a metaphysician? The poet's influence will always be sympathetic rather than intellectual. Lampman is one of those authors whose personal character counts for as much as his writings, because it is the basis of those writings; if he gave us no direct or searching criticism of human life, he gave us what is better, or at least more acceptable, a glance into his own mind. William Dean Howells says: "His pure spirit was electrical in every line." Few poets have told us so much about themselves and yet said so little on the subject. There is an atmosphere of thoughtful deference which betrays the modest man; and modesty becomes the wearer, especially when it comes from deep reflection and self-searching; in an age and a country where a sturdy and aggressive self-confidence is—naturally enough—a predominant characteristic, the moderate utterance has an added power for good.

To leave generalities and come to details. Such poems as "The Clearer Self," "To the Prophetic Soul," "The Better Day," "Sapphics," contain all there is of philosophy —a simple philosophy of courage and endeavour, of faith in the ultimate good.

> Each mortal in his little span
> Hath only lived, if he have shown
> What greatness there can be in man
> Above the measured and the known;

> How through the ancient layers of night
> In gradual victory secure,
> Grows ever with increasing light
> The energy serene and pure:

> The Soul that from a monstrous past
> From age to age, from hour to hour,
> Feels upward to some height at last
> Of unimagined grace and power.

The theory of a spiritual evolution parallel to the material comes no longer with the force of an original thought; but these verses have the charm of simplicity and directness and the earnestness of ripe conviction. I should like to refer briefly to the poem "Sapphics" which Dr. Logan, in an article published some time ago, has quoted in full and discussed almost minutely. In this the poet contemplates the beauty of the trees in autumn, and from their eternal strength and hope draws courage for his own spirit:

> Yet I will keep my spirit
> Clear and valiant, brother to these my noble
> Elms and maples, utterly grave and fearless,
> Grandly ungrieving.

The moral application is clear—he who runs may read; by turning it inward upon himself the writer avoids the effect of preaching, a practice altogether foreign to his character.

Of a different type is the poem called "The Woodcutter's Hut." Practically the same subject has been treated by Roberts under the title of "The Solitary Woodsman," and the different styles are characteristic of the two poets. Roberts' woodsman is the most shadowy outline; not the slightest attempt is made to develop human character. He blends completely with the woodland features, himself hardly more prominent, inarticulate but keen of sense, the first of the animals. In Lampman's poem the woodcutter fills the stage, and though he is too merely—

> The animal man in his warmth and vigour, sound hard
>   and complete,

yet he takes on an individuality which the woodsman of Roberts does not possess. To Lampman the hut of the woodcutter conjures up:

The sense of a struggling life in the waste and the mark of a soul's command,
The going and coming of vanished feet, the touch of a human hand.

Roberts, however, thinks only of the wild life which surrounds the woodsman, the owl, the chipmunk, and the sly bear "summer sleekened"; or of the various sounds of the forest, which he hears, the call of the blue-jay, the scurry of the woodmice, the moose's call, the laughter of the loon. As a work of art Robert's poem is certainly the finer. The short stanza and line, the simple direct phrase, are far more appropriate to the subject than the long cumbersome line chosen in Lampman's poem. But apart from difference in form the treatment is particularly characteristic. Roberts' handling of the theme is entirely objective: he does not reveal his own personality, which merges completely into his subjects; he becomes, for the nonce, himself a child of nature, alert of sense but chary of words, quick to analyze the sounds of the forest, but quite averse to analysis of thought and character.

And he hears the partridge drumming,
The belated hornet humming,
All the faint prophetic sounds
That foretell the winter's coming.

And the wind about his eaves
Through the chilly night-wet grieves,
And the earth's dumb patience fills him,
Fellow to the falling leaves.

On the other hand, Lampman's attitude is here and always that of the student—an extraordinarily keen and appreciative one but nevertheless a student. It follows then that he is more detached, has more the eye of the observer, in other words he interprets what he sees. And herein, I fancy, is to be found the chief reason why as a poet he has a firmer hold than Roberts upon the reading public. A city man by force of circumstances, he voices the inarticulate feelings and desires of city people who, however much they may actually incline to the "flesh-pots," always have at the back of their minds an inherited thirst for green fields and cool woods. In Lampman they find their own appreciation of these things deepened and magnified into reverence, strengthened by an uncommon intimacy with the wonders of nature, and voiced in language both dignified and musical.

SONNETS—Here and there in the third volume are a few descriptive sonnets which, however, should be considered with the others in the fourth division of the complete edition. This collection of sonnets would form in itself a valuable contribution to any literature. It would seem that the pentameter with its dignity and flexibility is the most suitable vehicle of Lampman's thought. Other metres he handles with success, but gives the impression of coming back to this favourite measure with relief. These sonnets vary in style and thought between the tranquillity of "Evening" and the righteous wrath of the "Modern Politician." Sometimes the Petrarchan type is taken, with a clear division between octave and sestet; more often, however, there is no definite break in the thought. Occasionally the Shakespearian form is chosen as in the case of "In the Wilds." This sonnet is worth quoting as echoing a certain note which is very insistent, the joy of sensitive soul in the primal strength and cleanness of the wild. All lovers of the trail will appreciate this sonnet.

> We run with rushing streams that toss and spume;
> We speed or dream upon the open meres;
> The pine woods fold us in their pungent gloom;
> The murmur of wild water fills our ears;

The rain we take, we take the beating sun;
The stars are cold above our heads at night;
On the rough earth we lie when day is done
And slumber even in the storm's despite.
The savage vigour of the forest creeps
Into our veins, and laughs upon our lips;
The warm blood kindles from forgotten deeps,
And surgest tingling to the finger tips.
The deep-pent life awakes and bursts its bands;
We feel the strength and goodness of our hands.

Since the sonnets are so important a feature of Lampman's work it might be well to classify some of the most characteristic in the form of a table. This is a kind of pedagogical exercise, but it has the advantage of giving a bird's-eye view.

EXTERNAL NATURE, DESCRIPTIVE	EXTERNAL NATURE, REFLECTIVE	HUMANITY
Evening	Voices of Earth	Outlook
Among the Orchards	On the Companion-	Aspiration,
A Thunderstorm	ship with Nature	The Modern Politician
Solitude	In the Pine Groves	Virtue
Indian Summer	The Passing of the	Stoic and Hedonist
After the Shower	Spirit	To an Ultra Protestant
A January Morning	In the Wilds	The Largest Life
Winter Uplands	Earth the Stoic	The Death of
	In Beechwood	Tennyson
	Cemetery	

Selection is difficult, and any choice is bound to be unsatisfactory. There is a uniformity about the sonnets which makes it nearly impossible to pick any outstanding examples. Nor is it possible to be arbitrary on the question of merit. Some of the purely descriptive poems are perfect works of art, landscapes in vignette; again, those in which the author's reflections on humanity form the main theme have a dignified simplicity and force which recall the sonnets of Wordsworth. Any choice among these must depend on the personal taste of the reader.

IV. POEMS AND BALLADS

The fifth and last division contains some miscellaneous poems and ballads, "The Story of an Affinity," in the style of Tennyson's country idylls, and a dramatic poem in three scenes, "David and Abigail," certainly offers proof of latent dramatic ability. The characterization of some of the slighter persons, especially of Joab and Miriam, is done with skill. But the subjective quality of Lampman's mind belongs more to the lyrical than the dramatic. His own reflections take shape in the words of his characters, which consequently have an impossible power of self-analysis. Making all allowances for poetical freedom, one cannot imagine Abigail, wife of Nabal, expressing herself like this:

> Our only happiness, our final joy
> Is in persisting calmly to the goal,
> And he who struggles from his ordered way,
> How hard so'er it be, even in thought,
> Reaps in the end but bitterness and shame.
> He only can be happy who is strong,
> Who bears above the crying tides of passion
> And movements of the blind and restless soul
> A forehead smooth with purpose, and a will
> Spacious and limpid as the cloudless morn.

Of the shorter poems, "The Passing of Autumn" has a dainty music and shows a more imaginative treatment than most of the woodland sketches. It has that pure lyric note, which is occasionally muffled in Lampman by a laborious carefulness of phrase.

> The wizard has woven his ancient scheme
> A day and a starlit night;
> And the world is a shadowy-pencilled dream
> Of colour, haze and light
>
> Like something an angel wrought, maybe
> To answer a fairy's whim,
> A fold of an ancient tapestry,
> A phantom rare and dim.

Slim as out of aerial seas,
The elms and poplars fair
Float like the dainty spirits of trees
In the mellow dream-like air.

Silvery-soft by the forest side
Wine-red, yellow, rose.
The Wizard of Autumn, faint, blue-eyed,
Swinging his censer, goes.

The most interesting and certainly the most vigorous
of the ballads is "Phokaia," describing the wanderings of
the inhabitants of that ancient city of Ionia. The Phokaeans, after the conquest of Ionia by the Persians, refused
to submit to their tyrant, Harpalus, and gathering their
household goods set sail for new lands:

Dear are the seats of our gods, and dear is the name
Of our beautiful land, but we will not hold them with
      shame.
Let us take to the ships, for the shores of the sea are wide
And its waves are free and wherever our keels shall ride
There are sites for a hundred Phokaias.

Fate was against them, the lands they visited were hostile,
and their fleet was attacked by the Carthaginians; however, the Phokaeans won the day, though badly shattered,
and the remnant came, with fortunate winds and omens,
to "a little port on a sunny rock-built shore." From this
germ rose the city of Massilia, the modern Marseilles. The
rugged strength and independence of this handful of sea-
faring Greeks seems to have been perpetuated in their
descendants, the Marseillais, who gave to France her
national song of liberty.

In conclusion, both Lampman and Roberts, by the
volume of their work and by its general excellence, stand
well in the front of Canadian nature poets. They are both
truly Canadian, products of the soil. While the range of
Roberts is broader, his treatment more varied and his

scholarship more thorough, Lampman has the more intimate appeal, through that personal element which, though not always directly expressed, is keenly felt behind all he wrote. The difference might be expressed in this way: while Roberts gives us beautiful impressions of Nature, Lampman interprets her. His is the Spirit of Solitude of whom Shelley wrote:

> Every sight
> And sound from the vast earth and ambient air
> Sent to his heart its choicest impulses.

His verses, whether purely descriptive or containing some moral reflection, invariably have that element of thoughtfulness which gives them a value below the surface. Further, his exactness of detail is educative and stimulates to a keener interest in Nature. Let any reader take one of the long poems of the seasons, such as "The Meadow," "Comfort of the Fields," "April," "June," "September," carefully verify the different features there introduced. If he can do so without learning something new and interesting he will be either a Philistine or a biologist. Mr. Wilfred Campbell, in an aggressive mood, makes it out to be quite a merit in himself that he does not know the names of flowers and birds. He thinks such exact technical knowledge is a sign of poetic degeneracy. It reminds one of the story of a convivial Keats who drank "Confusion to Newton," because he had destroyed "the poetry of the rainbow." But Keats was a disciple of the romantic and the unreal. There will always be this conflict in poetry between prosaic reality and ethereal fancy. The task of the modern poet clearly is to lift the prosaic to the divine, to live among realities and to ennoble them, not as Tennyson's artistic and selfish Soul in the Palace of Art, to build himself a house of "God-like isolation." Now, as to the application of this to the subject. Lampman, in his nature verse, has this accuracy of detail which brings him close to the way of modern life; "realistic" in the accepted sense

of the word he never is, since his pictures are always beautiful, his music is always sweet. It is to be admitted that in
a few of the longer poems there is a certain heavy luxuri-
ance, a monotonous sweetness, which detracts from their
artistic excellence. Here and there also he may lavish himself upon themes unworthy of much effort. But these are
natural blemishes, exaggerations of that fundamental
quality which gives him his peculiar charm, the quality
of soundness, the desire for truth in his art.

As a poet of humanity Lampman has not the direct
contact with life which characterizes his nature verse. He
is essentially a dreamer, projecting his mind into the past
or the future but avoiding the present. What ethical significance he develops is confined to the broader simpler
human issues, which are common to all ages. Always the
champion of simplicity, honesty and courage, the primal
virtues, he has Matthew Arnold's contempt for Philistinism, the smug complacency which a prosperous com-
mercialism assumes; but his cheerful temper refuses to
accept the melancholy strain which tinges so much of that
great writer's verse. He sometimes bursts out passionately
against the narrowness of business or political life, and his
"Modern Politician" is as near violence as so gentle a
spirit could come; but he never shows personal bitterness
but rather the indignation of a just man against flagrant
injustice. In the sonnets to "The Truth" and "An Ultra
Protestant," he protests against intolerance in everyday
life and in religion:

> Wisest is he who, never quite secure,
> Changes his thoughts for better, day by day;
> To-morrow some new light will shine, be sure,
> And thou shalt see thy thought another way.

But it is not by isolated expressions that we arrive at
the mind of the man. To quote his friend and fellow poet,
Mr. Duncan Campbell Scott, "Behind all he said and
wrote was felt a great reserve of wisdom and integrity."

There is an undercurrent of courage and kindliness, which does not expend itself in surface froth, but sends up an occasional strong swirl from the depths. Mr. Campbell's poem in his memory—"Bereavement of the Fields"—is a beautiful tribute and will surely take its place among the great elegies. It is old-fashioned to conclude with a verse; but no words could sum up more fitly the essence of Lampman's genius:

> Songs in our ears of winds and flowers and buds
> And gentle lives and tender memories,
> Of Nature's sweetest aspects, her pure moods,
> Wrought from the inward truth of intimate eyes
> And delicate ears of him who harks and broods,
> And, nightly pondering, daily grows more wise
> And dreams and sees in mighty solitudes.

THE POETRY OF ARCHIBALD LAMPMAN

RAYMOND KNISTER

Though a new and perhaps final volume of the selected poems of Archibald Lampman has recently appeared, his work is of the sort which does not depend upon seasonal notice. More, perhaps, than that of any other Canadian poet, it is objective; and his vignettes of the outward Canadian scene will always have a present value, if an historic one. Indeed Lampman wrote of natural circumstance with such care in observation, such faithfulness of tone and almost submissiveness of mood, that his readers might be

"The Poetry of Archibald Lampman," by Raymond Knister. In *Dalhousie Review* 7 (October 1927), 348-61. By permission of the Estate of Raymond Knister.

excused for forgetting or scarcely perceiving the definite relation he bore to the life and the thought of his time in general. We see in the admirable Introduction by his friend and fellow-poet, Duncan Campbell Scott, that his life was not without storm and stress, and yet for the majority of poetry-lovers his name evokes clear and tranquil pictures of the Canadian countryside.

Long furrows, steaming horses in the sun, a stump shorn of surrounding grass, quaint crows filling the forest with din, pines—"tall slim priests of storm"—snowbirds like tossing spray, piping frogs, the nearness of spring sounds, beardlike rows of icicles below cabin eaves, the eternal little speedwell in the grass, the vesper-sparrow's song, the roar of rapids in the dark, the path of the moon across water, the wild raspberry, blueberry, juniper, spikenard, trees and their shadows, the lift of hills, the peace of lakes, drive of rivers, "the wind, the world-old rhapsodist," and again the cherry cheeks of lumberjacks and teamsters, the squeaking runners of sleighs bearing logs and cordwood!

Of these matters, with the undertone or obligato of his own moods, Archibald Lampman formed his poems. It was Canada, reproduced in a spirit sensitive and open to new impressions, rendered with unassuming artistic certainty. So clearly was this the case that recognition was not long in coming, and the best of incentives, the regard of his fellow-workers. "Lampman never worked in loneliness or without appreciation," writes Dr. Scott. "He might feel that his soul was parched by routine, but he never felt that other desolating consciousness that no one heeded or comprehended him." Yet perhaps this lack of tension between the poet and his environment was the element which kept him from development in the measure of those possibilities which became plain in him toward the end of his life. We are not concerned with failure here, but with the question why Lampman, with his elements of greatness and his artistic discipline, did not, even in his thirty-eight years, become a great poet.

He was born in 1861, of six national blood-strains, French, Dutch, German, Swiss, Scottish and English, at Morpeth, Kent County, Ontario. The combination of racial tendencies, Celtic temperament and Saxon endurance, which had produced in his family adventurous and sedentary types—Loyalist stock—made Lampman what he was, and gave him an unusual balance of qualities. His father was a clergyman of the Church of England, so that he early experienced the life of a number of small communities. These changes, however, did not seem to stimulate the proclivities of a connoisseur so much in human character as in the outer forms of nature. The study and the field seem to have occupied his days. His father, moreover, with a fondness for what was called *belles lettres*, adhered to the critical faiths of the eighteenth century. The Augustan age of English literature had produced Dryden and Pope as its poetical prototypes, and there had been Addison and Fielding; it was an age civilized, lifeloving, more brutal and more formal than others before and since. Though the young poet in effect rebelled against such tenets and repudiated such heroes, he was affected by them, even as he turned to the more transcendental Shelley and Keats and Wordsworth. If he seemed to lean too heavily upon these latter, it may be recalled that the generations moved more slowly then, and that the distance of Kent County from England counted for more. Moreover, literature is always considerably a matter of fashion, and young poets in such places still write from Tennyson and Arnold, proportionately no more remote from their own experiences. Hence the peculiar fusion of qualities in Lampman's muse—since the form of poetry was primarily a function of taste. Though he lived in the later part of the Victorian age, he was not primarily a Victorian.

Lampman entered Trinity College, Toronto, in 1879, and graduated in 1882. It is plain that the state of Canadian culture at this time was peculiar. The feeling of isolation, of the impossibility of emulating classical achievement, and the consequent delight and triumph in any attempt to break what seemed to amount to a spell, may be described by himself. He is referring to the first volume of poetry published by Charles G. D. Roberts:

One May evening somebody lent me *Orion and Other Poems,* then recently published. Like most of the young fellows about me, I had been under the depressing conviction that we were situated hopelessly on the outskirts of civilization, where no art and no literature could be, and that it was useless to expect that anything great could be done by any of our companions, still more useless to expect that we could do it ourselves. I sat up most of the night reading and re-reading *Orion* in a state of the wildest excitement, and when I went to bed I could not sleep. It seemed to me a wonderful thing that such work could be done by a Canadian, by a young man, one of ourselves. It was like a voice from some new paradise of art, calling us to be up and doing.

Perhaps had there not been a group of writers at this time, Scott, Roberts, Carman, E. W. Thomson, W. W. Campbell and Lampman, the work of none of these men individually should have had the definite qualities which it possessed. This country was legitimately a province of England, as culturally the United States was; and the normal response of a writer to his environment was that of a more or less thoroughly transplanted Englishman. It is obvious, moreover, that the audience to which he is addressing himself exerts a pressure of influence upon the artist, and that his work is really an adjustment made so that he can be understood, even when it is essentially self-expression. Hence came the peculiarities of much of the literary work of Lampman's time. To have accepted Canadian experience and written of Canada in terms of nothing else would have been, if not impossible, at least immediately fruitless and unrewarded. Life had not been going on long enough in Canada for many people to have a vivid

sense of it; and if they read, they hoped to see something
after the approved models of Europe. Later, of course,
came the cult of Canada as a scene of conventional romantic adventure. This was fostered by the public of other
countries, and still reverberates here. In Lampman's time
readers were so few that they could scarcely be reached
at all save through the daily newspapers, but had to be
approached by means of English and imitative American
publications. The group to which he belonged maintained
a balance between enthusiasm for their native land and
emulation of the accepted masters of English literature.

At best, accordingly, the poet in Canada did well to
keep his eye on the object, Canadian landscape, more
rarely Canadian character and situations; the eye of one
taught by all-too-few favourite English masters. Sometimes
such a one did not even keep his eye accurately upon the
object, and too often he lapsed into a weak-kneed banality
of line and a dependence upon the quality of recognition
in his reader. "That is good verse, it reminds me of
Shelley." It is not to be supposed that a poet of Lampman's
gifts would now begin a sonnet, "Beautiful are thy hills,
Wayagamack," or celebrate April in such strophes, fine in
their way, as

> Pale season, watcher in unvexed suspense,
> Still priestess of the patient middle day,
> Betwixt wild March's humoured petulance
> And the warm wooing of green kirtled May,
> Maid month of sunny peace and sober gray,
> Weaver of flowers in sunward glades that ring
> With murmur of libation to the spring;
>
> As memory of pain, all past, is peace,
> And joy, dream-tasted, hath the deepest cheer,
> So art thou sweetest of all months that lease
> The twelve short spaces of the flying year.
> The bloomless days are dead, and frozen fear
> No more for many moons shall vex the earth,
> Dreaming of summer and fruit-laden mirth.

To write in this way now would be equivalent to building one of those rambling, barrack-like houses once common to New England and our eastern landscapes, with fancy scrollings on the gables and the verandas. Such passing fads detract from basic and enduring qualities, in poetry truth of thought, integrity of feeling, and tempered expression, by which any structure outlasts the needs of one or two generations of men.

In Lampman's work we see a manifestation of the cult of nature, as it had become traditional since Roussseau and Goethe's *Werther* and Wordsworth; unabashed, despite a few dissenting voices, like Carlyle's bellow in *Characteristics*. Nature was not merely an inspiration to veracity and a high view of man—who is after all man's only subject—but an entity separate and outside of man and his manufactured concerns. Yet she was, contradictorily, a presiding goddess to whom he attributed his own qualities and even moods. Nature was calm and aloof, or tempestuous and moody with or in contrast with man; while, as a matter of fact, she is nothing of the sort, but simply nature. Man, according to such a criterion, was to turn to nature, not because he was so much man that he was kin to all creation, but because he was tired, sick with being man, and desirous of rest and a forgetting within a serene impersonality, a soothing power to which he could moreover assign his own tempers, "or wailful or divine."

Beyond this cult of nature for nature's sake, which has been the bane of gifts not vigorous enough to deal with experienced reality as a whole, Lampman was evolving. His acceptance of convention was mostly formal and tentative. He had a deep trust in reality, when others tended to fly to abstractions and idealizations. So it is a thing to be remarked that no poet has made clearer and more definite pictures, which are objective in the sense of meaning much the same to every reader, and at the same time has induced feeling, reported a fusion of the preconceived mood of

nature and that of the poet. The famous "Heat" is an
example of this, and among many others a stanza of "In
October":

> Here will I sit upon this naked stone,
>   Draw my coat closer with my numbed hands,
> And hear the ferns sigh, and the wet woods moan,
>   And send my heart out to the ashen lands;
> And I will ask myself what golden madness,
>   What balmed breaths of dreamland spicery,
> What visions of soft laughter and light sadness
>   Were sweet last month to me.

And poems like "In November," with plain statement and
occasional prosaic lines, often crystallize in a felicitous
naming of the poet's mood:

> A nameless and unnatural cheer,
> A pleasure secret and austere.

There was a passion for exactitude in description and in
the use of words which gives Lampman's work unusual
definiteness and outline. He had a real feeling for the
exterior world. Nor is the human figure always forgotten,
though met as seldom as in the walk through forests and
fields on a winter's day:

> Across a waste and solitary rise
>   A ploughman urges his dull team,
> A stooped gray figure with prone brow
>   That plunges bending to the plough
> With strong, uneven steps. The stream
>   Rings and re-echoes with his furious cries.

Such glimpses as these, brief as they are, show that Lampman was not writing from imagination of bucolic swains
in the pages of other poets, but from his own quite definite
observation. Most felicitous, for example, is the last stanza
of "By An Autumn Stream," which evokes a feeling

familiar to anyone who has experienced autumn in the open:

> All things that be
> Seem plunged into silence, distraught,
> By some stern, some necessitous thought:
> It wraps and enthralls
> Marsh, meadows and forest; and falls
> Also on me.

After graduation from Trinity College, Lampman took to teaching in a high school, but finding the profession uncongenial, entered the Civil Service in Ottawa, in the Post Office Department, in 1883. This post he occupied until his death in 1899. It is curious that one of our earliest poets, and one dedicated to the aspects of newness, should for his virtues be sentenced to sedentary routine. This influence of such a life upon one given to the joys of the fields and the study was bound to make itself felt in the course of years. There is little feeling of frustration or maladjustment apparent in Lampman's poetry, and yet it existed in his life. He intended to remain with the Civil Service until 1899, the year in which he died, and then he intended if possible to be superannuated and, retiring to the country, to devote himself to poetry. The amount of annual income necessary for this course was still less at that time than it is now, but the thing was not be be compassed, Lampman failed in health, and in brief it may be said that Canada allowed her poet to die. In 1895 he wrote:

I am getting well weary of things. I was so far gone in hypochrondria on Saturday last that I had not the spirit to go to my office at all. I went straggling up the Gatineau Road, and spent the whole day and most of the next under the blue sky and the eager sun; and then I began to perceive that there were actually trees and grass and beautifully loitering clouds in the tender fields of heaven; I got to see at last that it was really June, and that perhaps I was alive after all.

By the following year he had reached a philosophy of desperation, no longer caring about his fortunes, having "given up for good and all the notion of writing anything large or important." It was necessary for every man to ascertain his capabilities and his relation to the world, and adjust himself accordingly. "All our troubles in reality proceed from nothing but vanity, if we track them to their source. We form an ideal of ourselves, and claim what seems to be due to that ideal. The ideal of myself is entitled to love and approbation from my fellow-creatures: but the love and approbation does not appear, and I fret and abuse the constitution of things. To the ideal of myself money and power and practical success are no doubt due, but they do not come, and again I abuse the constitution of things."

This is playing the devil's advocate with a bitter vengeance. To any reasoning intelligence it is plain that Lampman was within his rights in abusing the constitution of things. Seeing how this country lavished and continues to lavish prosperity upon men whose services, not always to call them such, could more easily be dispensed with, and seeing that it is because of a few men like Lampman that civilizations are remembered, it appears unfair that he could not have been rewarded with the right to live.

But if the opportunity of fulfilling his gift and the nature with which he was endowed was denied him, there were compensations, and there was growth of a kind. While the routine monotony of his day's work went on, and its lack of event acted as a pall to the quick spirit of poetry, it was chiefly the lack of leisure which prevented Lampman from doing his best work. Perhaps his sense of life was heightened by the very circumstances which made expression of it so difficult. Dr. Scott in the Introduction says finely: "The life of poetry is in the imagination; there lies the ground of true adventure, and though the poet's imagination may be starved and parched by the lack of variety in life, he persists nevertheless to make poetry out of its dust and ashes, out of its lets and hindrances, and even greatest poetry out of the small frets and sorrows that he shares with all mankind." As time went on, Lampman's writing, which had concerned itself with endeared natural objects, widened to include the major human emotions, and there even appeared a sense of character, if not of psychological subtlety. While it is unlikely that he would ever have rivalled Browning, he probably would have developed this side of his nature as time went on. It would be interesting to know, for example, whether "The Cup of Life" and "Personality" were not written in the order in which I quote them:

> One after one the high emotions fade:
> Time's wheeling measure empties and refills
> Year after year; we seek no more the hills
> That lured our youth divine and unafraid,
> But swarming on some common highway, made
> Beaten and smooth, plod onward with blind feet,
> And only where the crowded crossways meet
> We halt and question, anxious and dismayed.
> Yet can we not escape it; some we know
> Have angered and grown mad, some scornfully laughed;
> Yet surely to each lip—to mine, to thine—
> Comes with strange scent and pallid poisonous glow
> The cup of Life, that dull Circean draught,
> That taints us all, and turns the half to swine.

This explicit doubt and misgiving before life becomes a more quiet sense of its mystery in "Personality":

> O differing human heart,
> Why is it that I tremble when thine eyes,
> Thy human eyes and beautiful human speech,
> Draw me, and stir within my soul
> That subtle ineradicable longing
> For tender comradeship?

It is because I cannot all at once,
Through the half-lights and phantom-haunted mists
That separate and enshroud us life from life,
Discern the nearness or the strangeness of thy paths,
Nor plumb thy depths.
I am like one that comes alone at night
To a strange stream, and by an unknown ford
Stands, and for a moment yearns and shrinks,
Being ignorant of the water, though so quiet it is,
So softly murmurous,
So silvered by the familiar moon.

Such realization came but seldom, almost as infrequently as his use of free verse, so that such a fine evocation of the interwoven strands of fate as we find in "The Railway Station" is scarcely representative, but the more to be valued:

The darkness brings no quiet here, the light,
No waking: ever on my blinded brain
The flare of lights, the rush, and cry, and strain,
The engine's scream, the hiss and thunder smite;
I see the hurrying crowds, the clasp, the flight,
Faces that touch, eyes that are dim with pain:
I see the hoarse wheels turn, and the great train
Move labouring out into the bourneless night.
So many souls within its deep recesses,
So many bright, so many mournful eyes:
Mine eyes that watch grow fixed with dreams and guesses;
What threads of life, what hidden histories,
What sweet or passionate dreams and dark distresses,
What unknown thoughts, what various agonies!

But it is usually to escape from such matters, and the too-exigent pressure, that Lampman turns to nature, walking in field and wood:

Ah! I was weary of the drifting hours,
    The echoing city towers,

The blind gray streets, the jingle of the throng,
  Weary of hope that, like a shape of stone,
Sat near at hand without a smile or moan,
  And weary most of song.

So it came about that, instead of a pure delight in external
nature, which had informed the substance of June with
its tranquil and lovely lines, "Heat" and "Morning on
the Lievre," flawless in their way with a few slight perfect
words, we find him talking of "doubt and care, the ghostly
masters of this world"; and when he would escape, he is
burdened with a "soul shaped to its accustomed load of
silly cares and microscopic dreams." There are signs that
for Lampman nearly every city was "The City of the End
of Things," where "Flit figures that with clanking hands
obey a hideous routine. And from their iron lips is blown
a dreadful and motonous cry"—a terrific vision of the end
of a mechanistic era. This poem, because of its enigmatic
and nightmare quality, is more impressive than more
explicit plaints like "The City":

  Canst thou not rest, O city,
    That liest so wide and fair?
  Shall never an hour bring pity,
    Nor end be found for care?

In "Chaucer" he mourns for the passing of hearty and
oblivious days, and sees that now "too well we see the drop
of life lost in eternity." He finds the hunger of Xeno-
phanes still preying on the hearts of men who probe "the
same implacable mysteries," who toil and "bear the same
unquenchable hope, the same despair."

Yet this very attitude, which might be construed as a
puritanic doubt of life which largely made life what it
was at that period, developed into a higher and larger
conviction, which is only now beginning to reach the

minds of the generality of men. It can best be expressed by Lampman himself:

This conception is the child of science, reinforced by the poetry that is inherent in the facts of the universe and all existence. Thus reinforced, the conception is a religious one. It is independent of the ancient creeds, for it does not trust for its effects to any system of post mortem rewards and punishments. It is different from the old Stoic virtue of the philosophers, which at bottom was merely prudence, a utilitarian quality. This modern conception is not a materialistic one, although at first it may seem so; it is, as I have said, poetic and intrinsically religious. It comes to those whom the new knowledge has made acquainted with the vast facts and secrets of life, arming them with a breadth and majesty of vision which withers away from the soul the greeds and lusts and meannesses of the old, narrow and ignorant humanity. The small ambitions and petty passions of this world seem infinitesimal indeed to him who once enters into the new conception and lives, as it were, in the very presence of eternity. As yet this new spiritual force acts only upon the few, for it is a modern thing, but its growth is sure. Spreading downward, with the steady extension and dissemination of culture, from mass to mass, it may in the end work its way into the mental character and spiritual habit of all mankind. Then indeed the world will become less and less a hospital, and the old cankerous maladies gradually decline and disappear.

In the same gradual way, one feels, this conception of life would have permeated the conscious mind and the spirit of Archibald Lampman, and taken the outward form of more poetry to measure with the finest which he left; and perhaps work finer, even in the most adverse circumstances, than any which he was privileged to do. There was a balance of qualities in his gift rarely to be found in a poet; and while this conception would have taken its part in all that he wrote, he would not have forgotten that poetry is to make things real—those of the imagination, and of the tangible world: "simple, sensuous and passionate" were the words with which Milton described poetry. He would not have become bogged in moral preoccupations as Wordsworth was, nor on the other hand would he have found the be-all and end-all in the senses, as Swinburne did. His art was controlled, and conscious. Dr. Scott tells us how he first wrote the last two lines of Winter Uplands:

> Though the heart plays us false and life be bare,
> The truth of Beauty haunts us everywhere.

This creditable but quite extraneous sentiment was changed to the objective completion of the present version.

In truth it must be admitted that there was little of lyric excess and abandon, little of any kind of excess, in Lampman's muse. He delighted in June days and January mornings, but it was a mild delight. The note of zest is struck infrequently, as in "In the Wilds," where "The savage vigour of the forest creeps into our veins, and laughs upon our lips," and the measures of "April in the Hills":

> I feel the tumult of new birth;
> I waken with the wakening earth;
> I match the bluebird in her mirth;
>   And wild with wind and sun,
> A treasurer of immortal days,
> I roam the glorious world with praise,
> The hillsides and the woodland ways,
>   Till earth and I are one.

This is contradistinct from inspired description such as we find in "The Piano":

> Low brooding cadences that dream and cry,
> Life's stress and passion echoing straight and clear;
> Wild flights of notes that clamour and beat high
> Into the storm and battle, or drop sheer;

> Strange majesties of sound beyond all words
> Ringing on clouds and thunderous heights sublime;
> Sad detonance of golden tones and chords
> That tremble with the secret of all time. . . .

Typical is the poem "In May," where the poet, overborne by grief the night before, and aware that his lot may be the same tomorrow, finds distraction and an "hour of blessedness" by entering into the manifold life of birds, sowers, rivers, roads, and trees. He prays to Earth, "the mother who was long before our day" for "Some little of thy light and majesty." And in her voices he finds that

> To him who hears them, grief beyond control,
> Or joy inscrutable without a name
> Wakes in his heart thoughts bedded there, impearled,
> Before the birth and making of the world.

Lampman's feeling was deep and genuine, his sight unusually clear, and what from any point of view could be called lapses are rare. He found in the wind a brother and in the voice of frogs the voice of "earth our mother." He moaned, "O Life! O Life! . . . . And the very word seemed sad," until he heard a veery, when "the very word seemed sweet." His goal was

> song,
> Whose substance should be Nature's song, clear and
>   strong,
> Bound in a casket of majestic rhyme.

And on the other hand such ruling moderation seldom became actually austere. "Sapphics" gives such an embodiment to an oft-repeated conception of the relation of nature and human destiny, as far as could be wished from jingling banality:

Clothed in splendour, beautifully sad and silent,
Comes the autumn over the woods and highlands,
Golden, rose-red, full of divine remembrance,
          Full of foreboding.

Soon the maples, soon will the glowing birches,
Stripped of all that summer and love had dowered them,
Dream, sad-limbed, beholding their pomp and treasure
          Ruthlessly scattered:

Yet they quail not: Winter with wind and iron
Comes and finds them silent and uncomplaining,
Finds them tameless, beautiful still and gracious,
          Gravely enduring.

Me too changes, bitter and full of evil,
Dream by dream have plundered and left me naked,
Gray with sorrow. Even the days before me
          Fade into twilight.

Mute and barren. Yet will I keep my spirit
Clear and valiant, brother to these my noble
Elms and maples, utterly grave and fearless,
          Grandly ungrieving.

Brief the span is, counting the years of mortals,
Strange and sad; it passes, and then the bright earth,
Careless mother, gleaming with gold and azure,
          Lovely with blossoms—

Shining with anemones, mixed with roses,
Daisies mild-eyed, grasses and honeyed clover—
You and me, and all of us, met and equal,
          Softly shall cover.

Sometimes it is possible to judge the position of a writer,
or that he would prefer to occupy, and his judgment of
his own capabilities, by his ideal among the masters who
have gone before. In the case of Lampman we find that
his prevailing temperate quality and his search for the
happy medium led him to find a poet on the highest plane

in Matthew Arnold, rather than others of his age who embodied desperate qualities in a more extreme manner. "The whole range of life, time and eternity, the mysteries and beauties of existence and its deepest spiritual problems are continually present to his mind. In his genius is that rare combination of philosophy and the poetic impulse in the highest degree which has given us our few solitary poets." Yet this ideal of nobility does not close Lampman's eyes to reality, and we find him painting this deeply shaded caricature of "The Poets":

> Half god, half brute, within the self-same shell,
> Changers with every hour from dawn till even,
> Who dream with angels in the gate of heaven,
> And skirt with curious eyes the brinks of hell,
> Children of Pan, whom some, the few, love well,
> But most draw back, and know not what to say,
> Poor shining angels, whom the hoofs betray,
> Whose pinions frighten with their goatish smell.
> Half brutish, half divine, but all of earth,
> Half-way 'twixt hell and heaven, near to man,
> The whole world's tangle gathered in one span,
> Full of this human torture and this mirth:
> Life with its hope and error, toil and bliss,
> Earth-born, earth-reared, ye know it as it is.

This brings us logically to the subject of Lampman's sonnets. The qualities which he most admired when expressed in brief compass find their best form in the sonnet, while the discipline of the form was one which, sympathetic to him, he did not allow to become too rigid. In the remainder of his work metrical experiments are few, and we seldom find him seeking a variant in poetic expression to suit his own needs. Accordingly it is not surprising to find that the sonnets, of which there are more than a hundred, when taken as a unit, constitute the most impressive portion of Lampman's work. This strictest

and most exigent of poetic forms awkward in the hands
of any save the most expert, and unsatisfying frequently
with them, he made into an expressive medium of his own.
Crisp, apparently bare sentences build a firm structure, a
clear picture, a moment of emotional realization. Like
most simplicity, it is deceptive; the reader's attention is
seldom strained more than by reading a newspaper paragraph. While as for the vague, irrelevant sublimity which
is usually drawn from the sonneteer by the demands of
rhyme in the way that evidence is drawn from a witness
by a cross-questioning lawyer, it is in Lampman generally
absent. In pictorial quality these sonnets remind one of
clear water-colours, and the even excellence of picture in
like number and quality seldom has been equalled. They
form in their sort a body of work which will not suffer by
any legitimate comparison. It is no small merit, if a negative one, that of few other poets in any age can it be said
that they wrote so few meretricious lines.

Not to quote one of these sonnets is impossible; and it
is almost as difficult, if one has known Lampman's work
for long, to apply purely critical judgment. Therefore
"Evening" may be taken, not as representing the best, but
an old personal predilection:

> From upland slopes I see the cows file by,
> Lowing, great-chested, down the homeward trail,
> By dusking fields and meadows shining pale
> With moon-tipped dandelions. Flickering high,
> A peevish night-hawk in the western sky
> Beats up into the lucent solitudes,
> Or drops with griding wing. The stilly woods
> Grow dark and deep, and gloom mysteriously,
> Cool night wings creep, and whisper in mine ear,
> The homely cricket gossips at my feet,
> From far-off pools and wastes of reed I hear,
> Clear and soft-piped, the chanting frogs break sweet
> In full Pandean chorus. One by one
> Shine out the stars, and the great night comes on.

And "Late November"; though many of the sonnets were not professedly landscapes:

> The hills and leafless forests slowly yield
> To the thick-driving snow. A little while
> And night shall darken down. In shouting file
> The woodmen's carts go by me homeward wheeled,
> Past the thin fading stubbles, half concealed,
> Now golden-gray, sowed softly through with snow,
> Where the last ploughman follows still his row,
> Turning black furrows through the whitening field.
> Far off the village lamps begin to gleam,
> Fast drives the snow, and no man comes this way;
> The hills grow wintry white, and bleak winds moan
> About the naked uplands. I alone
> Am neither sad, nor shelterless, nor gray,
> Wrapped round with thought, content to watch and
>   dream.

Lampman may be figured as in his poem, one listening in the darkness, stirred by all the currents of life in a wind, and its changelessness in a moon. The forces of life, the primary emotions were present to him; and if individual character and interactions of temperament were a trifle misty, that was perhaps the defect of his merits, the price of his poetic qualities. There are signs, too, that give the measure of a growth which his years were not to fulfill before he died. But he passed "with creative eye" over the country which the farmer and the lumberman and the railway-builder had possessed, and reaped another, more enduring harvest. What he left as heritage will long mean "Canada" in the minds of his countrymen, as surely as her fields and lakes were Canada to him.

CANADIAN WRITERS OF THE PAST—V:
ARCHIBALD LAMPMAN

LEO KENNEDY

Archibald Lampman shares with Canada's few other talented poets, and most of her untalented ones, the ill-luck to have been written about in terms of excessive nonsense. If his position in what the incautious are pleased to call Canadian literature is falsified, if a four-square evaluation of his work is as yet unforthcoming, the fault may be only partly laid to the poet himself. The chief offenders have been those well-meaning but overbiased friends of Lampman who have permitted themselves hearty splurges into adulatory print, and the leisured, patriotic persons whose self-appointed task it is to create legendary beings and national figures.

For that matter, as long as Canadian writers continue to contract for each other's washing, the critical truth about Canadian literature will be very hard to come by. Whether D. C. Scott and Archibald Lampman scratch each other's backs in '99, or A. M. Klein and Leo Kennedy pick fleas off each other in '33, the principle remains uncomfortably the same, though the phrasing of the interred generation with its coy cupidons and floral fixings, has assumed latter-day roughneck characteristics.

But because the convention has it that talent is discovered, not born, because an artist's intimates are usually more eager and liable, though possibly least qualified to summarize his ability, this problem of log-rolling presents

"Canadian Writers of the Past: Archibald Lampman," by Leo Kennedy. In *Canadian Forum* 13 (May 1933), 301-03. By permission of the author.

a quite embarrassing dilemma. As literary values are disruptingly relative at best, and as Canadian criticism is too dependent on digestion and similar un-literary influences (Mr. Stephen Elyot's excellent essay "Science and Criticism" has made this painfully clear), the honest sceptic can only hope that the generation-after-next will estimate his contemporary with unfalsified weights. Though these as yet unlicensed critics in their turn may be reactionarily spleened and bigoted in a way that will reflect credit on their predecessors' urbanity. . . .

It is all very puzzling.

And it does not help poor Lampman much. Nevertheless, it is a detailed way of saying that the rash panegyrics of "Canada's Great Poet of Nature," i.e., Archibald Lampman, may be no more outrageous than today's increasing arguments for his demotion, nor than the restorative monographs which a more obliging posterity will write on him in 1966, when tastes and fashions in poetry undergo another scheduled, cyclic revolution.

Archibald Lampman then—to resume loosened ends— has been too long and too loudly publicized as John Keats' little Canadian brother, with literary kinship to Wordsworth on the tedious side. He has been piously elevated for his idealism, and endlessly whooped for his cinematographic studies of nature. Excessive copy has been made of the fact that he hailed indirectly from the Maritimes— Canada's cradle of literary humanity—and issued from strictly Royalist stock. Like the late Bliss Carman, his name and work have been seized upon by patriotic women's groups, hot for national cultural advancement at any cost. Individuals who appear to have read no literature, but who pronounce the phrase "Canadian literature" as so much efficacious abracadabra, have made great hay by reading singularly ill-chosen sonnets from *Lyrics of Earth* at writers' clubs, mothers' meetings, and as entrée between the soup and roast at business men's boost rallies. In brief, he has been much ill used.

And yet, as implied above, not altogether without blame. For the legendary figure of Lampman, made in the image and likeness of the conventional "poet" of the last century, a hater of cities, crowds, etc., a worshipper of nature, an advocate of extremely simple living and very high ideals, a solitary dreamer of dreams which are never defined or described . . . in short, a seclusive, paranoiac person . . . this figure, I say, has been aided and abetted by Lampman himself in his poems. The posture has unfortunate connotations, since it is usually accompanied by poetic vapidity. It is invariably found in the opera of the open-road-and-space cult of Canadian versifiers. It is sham-heroic and unadmirable. And it was the dominant note in our poetry up till a couple of decades ago.

What are the qualities of this insularity? It is exemplified by intellectual sterility; a lack of interest in contemporary activity and development; and an unwillingness to make contacts outside of the immediate, provincial little sphere.

These are not in themselves disqualifications to pure poetry, nor are they beyond the personal privilege of a poet. He may write enduring verse with no preoccupations other than those three cardinal staples of the poet's repertoire, love, life, and death. He may live through a revolution of blood and rapine, and write only pastorals, yet be well within his rights. He may, if he cares to, perch on a boulder of Ararat like some inhospitable Noah, oblivious of his contemporaries and their efforts at creative salvation. But he must bring to his work some compensatory qualities.

If a poet is to limit his subject matter to one or two bald and unforgettable truisms, that we live, for example, and that we die, he must be able to contribute his own acceptable variations of these themes. If, as in the case of Lampman, he concentrates mainly on the phenomena of nature, it is not enough to see them with sobriety and poeticalness. He must wring out a meaning that is both personal and universal. Then, for a poet to lack active social virtue may be felicitous and even wise. It does not presume in him less virtue than is discovered in those writers who have a social outlook, and who do not withdraw themselves from current movements and remediable wrongs. But it does presume that he has within himself a sufficiency of strength, vision, and emotional depth. In fine, the narrower the scope he permits himself, the stronger must be his intensity, the more profound his feelings, the greater his ability to communicate his findings.

I am not abusing Lampman because his ideas were commonplace. I am not taking him to task because his verse does not reflect Canadian politics of the '90s. I am not indignant because his sonnets give no intimation that he ever heard of his European contemporaries, of the dazzling, decadent yellow book crew, or of the Americans, Markham, Lizette Woodworth Reese, and great Walt of Brooklyn, yawping a few miles to the south. But I do say that, since his own personal aesthetic contribution was insufficient for the purposes of art, he should have broadened his canvas, and borrowed from sources that would have benefitted him more.

Lampman's biographers and commentators insist that his vocation was to sing the new country, the new-found land, and on this point if on few others, his work endorses their claims. Yet no one in his senses can say that an apprenticeship to Keats and Wordsworth was the right foundation for such a task.

Norman Gregor Guthrie in his essay, *The Poetry of Archibald Lampman* (Musson, Toronto) says that, "Lampman apparently believed himself in some sense a reincarnation of the spirit of Keats." That is a tall statement for any literary ostrich to bolt, though quite in line with the hard things that have been written about Lampman. If this is true, it may explain why the poet developed the Keats strain to the exclusion of others which are more sympathetic to his own talent. The austerity of Arnold, which appears to have swayed him for a time, is surely more in keeping with the man's reserved character, puritan background, and creative sparseness, than the riotous efflorescence of Keats' imagination; though Arnold, too, is no mentor for a pioneer.

Lampman described natural phenomena with graceful realism. He made trim little etchings of snowcapes, crows in flight, and hepaticas in season, with a skill that points to accurate observation and a sharp sympathy for such things. His knowledge of Canadian flora was acquired in no naturalist's handbook or seed catalogue; he knew and deeply loved the season's manifestations. No other Canadian poet has described the country scene with such meticulous detail, but for all his careful observation, little in the form of an emotional climax comes out of it. The late Raymond Knister in a few scattered poems of a few scattered impressions could catch the very spirit of his cornfield or plough land, yet use the minimum of data. For a fair analogy, consider the rural Quebec scenes of Krieghoff beside the landscapes of Morrice.

Lampman wrote in the poetic diction laid down by the second generation poets of the Romantic Revival, a diction with which we today are wholly out of touch and sympathy. It exposes the essential weakness of his verse. Stock abstractions such as beauty, sorrow, despondency, truth, freedom, avarice, and unrest set him off on rhetorical sprees, from which he returned, a little shamefacedly, I hope, to write the simple, honest, thumbnail sketches about snowbirds, timothy, orchards, and song sparrows that he really understood and cared about. His devotion to the rag-tags of the poet's dictionary—the methinks, lo's, o'ers, bemoans, gats, the second person singular, begones, yesternights and yestereves—is dispiriting and trying.

His preoccupation with a very ridiculous concept of the poet's place in the scheme of things is really laughable. Again and again in the collected poems he suggests that

the poet is a vague, witless creature who engages himself
in an intolerable amount of dreaming:—

> Wrapped round with thought, content to
> watch and dream.

> Beyond the tumult of the hills,
> And all the city's sound and strife,
> Beyond the waste, beyond the hills,
> I look far out and dream of life.

> For me the dream 'tis enough to know
> The lyric stress. . . .

One could go on indefinitely. The following quotation,
frequently produced as evidence of Lampman's excellence,
amply illustrates any number of my charges: it is addressed
to "Night":

> Come with thine unveiled worlds, O truth of night,
> Come with thy calm. Adown the shallow day,
> Whose splendours hid the vaster world away,
> I wandered on this little plot of light,
> A dreamer among dreams.

This "dreamer" business has been hailed to high heaven
by Comrade Guthrie.

Yet Lampman has at times, a felicity of phrasing, and
a mild flutter of genuine emotion is startled here and
there.

*   *   *

And the current generation of Canadian poets, of whom
I am a hobbling member, has chucked him out, neck,
crop, and rhyming dictionary. Our quarrel is, perhaps, not
so much with Lampman as with his time and poetic tradition. The pot-bellied, serene Protestantism of Victorian
England which still flourished in Canada during the spruce
youth of Edward, and which underlay Lampman's spiritual make-up, causes us to chafe. We are impatient of

reading into the face of nature the conservative policies
of an Anglican omnipotence. We are principally concerned with the poetry of ideas and emotional conflicts.
We have detected, as the Lampmans do not appear to have
done, that all is decidedly not right with the world; we
suspect that God is not in his Heaven. Uncertain of ourselves, distressed by our inability to clarify our relationship to these and comparative issues, we do not feel
superior to circumstances at all.

That is, doubtless, a reason why we reject Lampman
and his fellows as exponents of a second-hand poetic
inheritance which does not stand the harsh light of our
day. Why we are irritated beyond good manners by their
acceptance of a too-glib philosophy. Why we are over
prone to greet the versified manifestations of both inheritance and outlook with a Bronx cheer.

ARCHIBALD LAMPMAN

W. E. COLLIN

Archibald Lampman passed the years of his manhood in
a small city of fifty to sixty thousand souls, the nominal
capital of a geographical unit covering a tremendous area
but supporting only five million people and, in a political
sense, not as old as himself. Ottawa, once sneered at as "a
backwoods lumber village transformed into a political
cockpit," grew rapidly after Confederation. It enjoyed
viceregal prestige and some gaiety in the season, but it was

"Archibald Lampman," by W. E. Collin. In *University of Toronto
Quarterly* 4 (October 1934), 103-20. By permission of the author and
the publisher, University of Toronto Press.

still artistically and intellectually dull. A literary and scientific society and a progressive club were in existence, and there was always the Library of Parliament; but books were hard to come by, and Lampman and his associates, who complained of the prevailing drought, kept themselves informed of the flow of ideas in the outer world by reading the great English and American monthlies and quarterlies.

In Canada, journals of that class did not then exist. Several literary magazines were launched and collapsed. One, *The Week*, continued to shine during the whole of the Lampman period. For young writers, yearning for literary expression, there were few outlets. South of the frontier, in the early 'nineties, there were sixty-five millions of people with but half a dozen or so first-rate magazines, admission to which was, in the circumstances, difficult for a Canadian. Yet it was in the pages of *Scribner's* and the others that Canadians might follow the work of their compatriots. If Canadian writers crossed the border, it was not because they were renegades. If they remained in their own country, what was there but obscurity and poverty?

Canada's future was one of the "burning" questions of the time. The young writers, conscious that a Canadian literature was in gestation, felt that annexation by the United States would be tantamount to absorption and utter loss. Yet a colonial status was intolerable, and only an independent people, they believed, could produce a great literature. Thus it came about that they preached nationalism. They were all anxious to establish a local distinctiveness for Canada; and if we review the ideas and emotions current at the time, I think we shall conclude that this distinctiveness could not be intellectual, political, or religious.

Canada did not produce ideas; she imported them from England, who was still dazzled by her latest discovery, natural law. Scientific method invaded all the fields of man's knowledge. It made breaches in the ramparts of his beliefs, and the foundations of his faith seemed to be sapped. In the English-speaking world it was positivism and "higher criticism," not the philosophy of Schopenhauer, that cast a gloom over men's spirits and made the years 1885 to 1900 a period of depression and pessimism. The question of life's purpose and value, the apparent futility of all action and thought, troubled the minds of serious people so that they welcomed any prophet who promised relief from the pain of thinking and knowing. Sir Edwin Arnold's poetic life of Gautama had an extraordinary vogue, and Fitzgerald's translation of Omar Khayyam, which had come into the world very silently some years before, sprang suddenly into public attention in 1885 and maintained an immense popularity throughout the whole period.

Lampman was particularly severe on Sir Edwin, "one of the most elaborate poetical frauds that ever worked up a reputation by palaver and puffery." To understand the virulence of those words it might be enough to remember that they came from a man who had been brought up in the discipline of the church, in a colony which had a reputation for being God-fearing, loyal to a Protestant crown, and in no mood to tolerate heresy. It was the puritanical pulse of Ontario that fluttered under the rays of contemporary scientific scrutiny. Modern method was an abomination. Ontario felt towards evolution as she felt towards continental realism; and read with relief the works of Henry Drummond, for evolution could be made palatable by being interpreted as redemption.

Not only was Archibald Lampman born in Ontario; he was born attached to an Anglican church in Ontario. The boy who was to be the poet, grew up under the authority of spiritual, not natural law. But outside the walls of home, scientists and critics were challenging that authority; and although Lampman's spiritual intuitions were not likely to be repressed altogether, his fervour might be diverted, as indeed it was, from the puritanism of his fathers. When he was grown up, he not unnaturally fell under the authority of Matthew Arnold. Why? Arnold offered a way of escape at once from science and from Hebraism. "From Maine to Florida, and back again, all America Hebraises," he said. "Now, and for us, it is a time to Hellenise . . . for we have Hebraised too much." He preached such gentle virtues: sweetness and light. Out of the encircling gloom he would lead his lambs, away from vexatious problems and distressing pain, to the green pastures and still waters of literature that would do them good. Lampman, and many another who had been over-exposed to divine worship, was ready for Hellenism, the Hellenism of nineteenth-century dreamers.

What could a poet do? He might read what he liked. There was no harm, if he happened to be summering in Muskoka, in feeling tired of action and swearing to live in the hollow lotus-land "careless of mankind." No harm, coming home in the sleigh as the northern-lights shot their midnight arrows into the sky, in murmuring the words of the Persian Omar:

> We are no other than a moving row
> Of Magic Shadow-shapes that come and go
>   Round with the Sun-illumin'd Lantern held
> In Midnight by the Master of the Show.

No harm in reading Swinburne's naughty ballads. Yet it was not possible for a poet to arise in Ontario and publicly intone hymns to the lotus, the grape, or Our Lady of Pain.

What could a poet write about? There were the Greeks. Add Emerson's Oversoul; then imitations of other accepted poets like Browning; lastly, patriotic or historical subjects. The shocks and adjustments occasioned in the sensibility of a poet as he faced his age, the only vital subject, and one which would have given us a different kind of romanticism? Frankly no.

Patriotism was changing its complexion. It had meant

loyalty to Britain; but in the sons of colonists, with a belief in independence, the idea of loyalty was being transformed into reverence for the Canadian soil. This was a departure. It opened a way to what there is of uniqueness in the Canadian poets of the Lampman period: not ideas, not mysticism, not oratory, but the smell of the Canadian soil. Lampman spent some of his boyhood at Lakefield. No boy would ever forget the flavour of that delightful countryside; it would penetrate his body to the bone. What fascinates us in our present study is ridding away foreign growths till we get a view of the Canadian *terroir* in the natural light of Lampman's style.

Lampman's sensibility was Nordic;[1] from beginning to end he felt the northness of Canada. This was one reason why he read Longfellow and William Morris. Morris made Nordic epic literature known to England. Besides, he was a master goaded by the impulse to create beauty; he knew colour effects not as a poet only but as a craftsman who works with dyes. However ineffectual Lampman thought Morris as poet, he could not ignore that.

One is bound to write a "band of blue," "garland of lilies," "girdle as red as blood"[2] after reading Pre-Raphaelite poetry. But there were some traits in that art that were out of Lampman's frontier by our definition: one of them was the love passion. There were others, poetic anthropomorphism, symbolism, not so definitely out of his reach as a poet as they were out of fashion in an age of realism. Yet I feel that it was a question of power as well as fashion with Lampman. For example, he changed his opinion of Shelley radically. He discovered that Shelley lacked something which, for want of a better word, he called "the human." Perhaps. But "the human" was lip-homage to Arnold. If he had been true to himself he would have admitted that he could not endure the blaze of Shelley's imaginative splendour any longer.

[1]"The venerable old Scald," he named Whitman.
[2]*The Little Handmaiden*, 1886.

It is evident that he admired the natural and direct method in landscape painting; the direct, simple style. He caught Rossetti's idea of making sonnets for pictures; he clung to novel and pretty descriptions of place or scene. As soon as he got to Ottawa he wrote: "This is a place not of wind and flowers, 'Full of sweet trees and colour of glad grass,' but a place of chill fierce colds, full of rheumatism and damned snowstorms."

Such language may indicate a *volte-face* from Swinburne and dream-pictures towards naturalism, but the new picture from *Poems and Ballads* stuck with him. Nine years later it comes out again, this time in its original setting: "Now it is that in the long afternoons we dream of some place of wind and flowers, 'Full of sweet trees and colour of glad grass'." There was something memorable, at any rate, in Swinburne. Words and the sweet sound of words! J. E. Collins, for whom Lampman had a genuine affection, wrote in 1884: "About a thousand silly young men in this country repeat the following lines till they grow drunken and inspired: 'And his heart grew sad, that was glad, for his sweet song's sake,' and, inspired, they go away and endeavour to write in the same strain." I take it that Collins had heard the line about a thousand times and was quoting from memory: "And men sit sad that were glad for their sweet songs' sake."[3]

Lampman's appropriation of another poet's pictures and the gentle merging of them into the work in progress is very obvious in his "months." Keats' poetry, where Lampman could find Pre-Raphaelite fancy and gem-like colours applied to a perfectly healthy landscape, was never far behind. Watch the Keatsian effects:

Thy shape hath flashed upon me like no dream,
    Wandering with scented curls that heaped the breeze,
Or by the hollow of some reeded stream
    Sitting waist-deep in white anemones.

[3]Swinburne, *In Memory of Barry Cornwall*.

Only the things of Beauty shall endure.

. . . .

The loneliness, perplexity and pain.

. . . .

. . . the long draught emptied to the lees.

. . . .

Mist of gray gnats that cloud the river shore.

. . . .

The word "murmurous" drones through his verse and prose: "the Murmurous May-Day," "long-strewn river murmurous with mills," "murmurous summer morning," "quiet, murmurous April evenings." Especially in the earlier poems of *Among the Millet* (1888), Lampman is under the influence of Keats. We admire the many-coloured procession of long-trained substantives: "pale-weeded shadows," "serpent-spotted blades," "frosty-lidded reveries," "dusty-skirted lines," and a rare condensed metaphor: "panting fires." The pace is retarded for us to see a lady's eyes "Broad with all languor of the drowsy South." Lampman was unfaithful to his northern muse there.

While the song-sparrows sing "Their clear thin silvery tunes in leafless trees," there is hardly a thought of moving at all. This sensation of slowness is one of Lampman's original achievements. He produces the effect of opiate slowness by lines of leaden monosyllables:

The cool wind creeps and faint wood odours steal;

. . . .

The dry dead leaves flit by with their weird tunes;

or by languid words like "sad," "slow," "weary," "pensive," "drowsy," "dreaming," "moan:" The wet woods moan; the dead leaves break and fall."

The weird narrative of "The Monk" is charged with Keatsian atmospherics and with fragments of realism which indicate the way Lampman is to go. But before he attains the pure objectivity of the sonnets, he had a lot of superfluous adjectives and romantic clap-trap to get rid of: sobbings, poison, and melodramatic *boursoufflure*; and the old romantic hero who *goes* but does not *know*:

> Whither I go I know not, and the light
> Is faint before, and rest is hard to win.

Of this romantic baggage Lampman will keep, even in his most realistic pictures, certain effects of vagueness, "austere" beauty; in his landscapes there is often something "afar off," something "dusky," "gray"; and how often he says *many a* this and *many a* that!

There is a statement about beauty and truth which the world will not let die. If Keats had been writing prose, said Lampman, "he might have added that goodness is another synonym for both truth and beauty. The love of beauty is the love of truth and goodness." That proves how securely Lampman was held by the weighty morality of Arnold. Such foolishness was exposed, Professor Babbit reminds us,[4] as far back as the time of Helen of Troy, who was beautiful, but "neither good nor true." Lampman added goodness to Keats, as Arnold added virtue and character.

Nothing is gained, in a literary study, by insisting that Lampman believed in goodness, unless that belief is operative in his work; but it is within our purpose to examine how far he believed in Matthew Arnold. He believed with Arnold that a man's efforts should be directed towards perfecting his peculiar gifts; that a poet's business is to see life steadily and see it whole. "The poet attaches himself to no dream. He endeavours to see life simply as it is, and to estimate everything at its true value in relation to the universal and the infinite."[5] I imagine that whenever

---

[4] *Rousseau and Romanticism*, p. 357.
[5] Toronto *Globe*, April 2, 1892.

Lampman speaks of "the human," "the fine breath of life," "the warm human impulses within us," he is mindful of his master. He does this, after a certain date, when he writes in a general way about poets. "It is a noticeable fact that the greatest poets, those few who are eminent above the others for dignity and majesty of tone, have been men of affairs before they were poets." They actively participated in great national efforts, lived full lives. Had the Greek revolution called Byron earlier in life it might have made him another Milton. Rossetti was not a great poet because he had not "the masterly ability to enter into every variety of life . . . nor that cheerful manliness which is the sign and seal of genial mastership in verse." Arnold made it easy for Lampman to deny Shelley.

In a passage dictated by Arnold's "high seriousness," and in order to acclaim Arnold the greatest poet of his generation, he remarks:

It is not the brilliancy, the versatility, the fecundity or the ingenuity of a poet that makes him "great;" it is the plane upon which his imagination moves, the height from which he looks down, the magnitude of his ideas, the largeness of vision. . . . Arnold is not so triumphantly the poet as Tennyson, nor is he so various or so clever as Browning, but he looks from a grander height than either, his imagination has its natural abode in a diviner atmosphere. The whole range of life, time and eternity, the mysteries and beauties of existence and its deepest spiritual problems are continually present to his mind.

A reader comes from Browning and Tennyson to Arnold "and then he seems to have reached the hills. With a mind blown clear as by the free wind of heaven he surveys the extent of life." I leave the reader to his own impressions. The passage shows how far Lampman was carried by Arnold's rhetoric; to the point where he ceased to be aware that, from such a height, his own poetry was insignificant.

How far was it possible for him to see life whole or to

see it steadily, from the lofty hill where he would have built his house if fate had been kind?

There was a prospect of town and country.

Ottawa corresponded to Arnold's definition of "provincial." It could not claim to be the centre of anything except legislative authority. Ideas were stagnant there. After ten years of going and coming along its streets, seared by its gyrating and snoring, Lampman felt it to be the "end" of all things, the haunt of Philistines and Mother Earth's prodigal sons; under its walls and towers he was a slave chained to the wheels of "hideous routine." "The City of the End of Things"[6] has often troubled me. Here the poet has been forced off his direct route, into the entanglements of allegory. And I have wondered what could have been the experience of a man who wrote a poem like this, lurid with apocalyptic fires and dreadful fate.

The city and its towers, from his first acquaintance with it in 1883, had been a pretty pictorial accessory in his poems:

> Yon city glimmering in its smoky shroud.

. . . .

> Cupola and pointed tower,
> Darken into solid blue.

But in 1892 the city comes into the foreground:

> Canst thou not rest, O City,
>   That liest so wide and fair;
> Shall never an hour bring pity,
>   No end be found for care?

Then in 1894 it takes on vast and infernal proportions and becomes a nightmare city builded in the abysses of an northern Tartarus:

---

[6]*Atlantic Monthly*, March, 1894.

And only fire and night hold sway;
The beat, the thunder and the hiss
Cease not, and change not, night nor day.
And moving at unheard commands,
The abysses and vast fires between,
Flit figures that with clanking hands
Obey a hideous routine;
They are not flesh, they are not bone,
They see not with the human eye,
And from their iron lips is blown
A dreadful and monotonous cry.

It had fallen from virtue, for it had once been a city of
sunlight and fair voices that mighty men had built in their
pride:

But now of that prodigious race,
Three only in an iron tower,
Set like carved idols face to face,
Remain the masters of its power.

But some time, finally the slacking wheels shall stop and
the fires moulder out, and even these three powers shall
perish. Only one of that accursed state, a gigantic idiot,
guardian of the silent desolation, will still sit staring out
into the lightless north.

The city is an epitome of a mechanical universe which
rolls round without purpose, heart, or mind, grinding out
life and death mercilessly and forever. "The iron age"
and "the benumbing sound" must have been familiar
words to a disciple of Arnold. But Lampman's doom city
from which sweetness and light have departed, where the
trinity of powers are masters of men who are only ghosts
of robots, stolid as idols, hissing through their iron lips as
they clank the treadmill, has an even more immediate and
personal reference. He had been depressed, no doubt, by
the struggle for existence in a city and had read something
which had decided him to write the poem. To my mind

there is very clear evidence that "The City of the End of Things" was composed by a poet who had read "The City of Dreadful Night.[7]

Without enumerating the many similarities of phrase and picture, we may remark a certain development in one of the images: The seated figure of Melancholia in Durer's engraving, which Thomson had in mind, becomes a sphinx in "The City of Dreadful Night"; in Lampman's poem the sphinx is changed into a grim idiot, "a bulk that never moves a jot." There are great differences, of course, between the two poems, and an enormous difference in importance. Thomson's masterpiece is an elaborated composition throbbing with strange depths of feeling in all its episodes; whereas the city set in the leafless tracts of Tartarus is simply fantastic and mechanical beyond all human credence. "The human," which Lampman looked for in literature and by which he pretended to judge it, is entirely eliminated. He complained that verse in his day was "compelled to contain so much of turgid personal experience." His own experience, therefore, for the nonce, he caricatured. There is one solid and memorable line describing the effect of the venomed air on a mortal who might chance to find the city:

> His soul would shrivel and its shell
> Go rattling like an empty nut.

That is Lampman's addition to the poetry of the City of Dis. What it needs is the vitalizing spirit of intense human emotion. As we have hinted above, he used his emotional experiences. He may have been taught a certain reticence in their regard, but the fact may be noted that not only personal but universal human experiences tend to disappear from his poetry, and, in their stead, we are presented with pieces of landscape, composed after nature and

[7]It first appeared in 1874 and, like the *Rubaiyat*, created no fuss. In 1892 an American edition was published at Portland, Maine.

resembling wood-cuts in which the lines are so evenly and delicately traced as to make us forget the labour of execution, under the general impression of smoothness and grace.

Like a voice among dry bones he wails: "We believe neither in God, humanity, nor self." This was his cry: "How utterly destitute of all light and charm are the intellectual conditions of our people and the institutions of our public life! How barren! How barbarous!"

When the religious beliefs that had warmed men's hearts were shaken, when there was no resounding call to great deeds of statecraft or battle, when politics were rotten with boodling and gerrymandering, where could he turn for that "earthly human heartiness" and "neighbourly warmth of touch," that perfection he hankered for? To Chaucer's merry England, to Greece, to poetry? Out of the city into solitude and dreams, out of corruption into art's perfection.

From his own pen we are sufficiently informed of his disposition:

If you are like me you will spend most of the long quiet winter evenings with your feet disposed upon an opposite chair, a long-stemmed pipe between your teeth and some entertaining book of travels placed comfortably against your knee. . . .

Out on a country road, walking in a quiet and silent downfall of snow, when distances are veiled and hidden and my mind seems wrapped about and softly thrown in upon itself by a smooth and caressing influence, I become immersed in . . . depth and intensity of reflection.

Tobacco, books of travel, and country walks induced a condition of reverie which well-nigh became chronic; the word itself, or its cognates, occurs on most of the pages of *Among the Millet* (1888) and *Lyrics of Earth* (1895). The condition, however, changes from actual reverie to a mere use of the word. We have the effect of it in "An Athenian Reverie," a long poem full of the joy of human converse,

comradeship, and travel. Nowhere else in Lampman do
we meet with such characterization. What are "open" eyes
or "liquid" eyes compared with that merry girl's eyes
which were "Full of the dancing fire of wanton Corinth"?
Who is speaking in these lines?

> To me is ever present
> The outer world with its untravelled paths
> The wanderer's dream, the itch to see new things.

Tennyson's Ulysses? A young dreamer tethered to a plot
in Ontario, who had never been out of it except in books
and dreams, who yearned for freedom and life. "How full
life is, how rich!" he wrote. "How dull life is, how poor!"
he felt. No. The poise attained through multifarious
activities among men in many places was a dream. Greek
friends, the happy adventures of Grecian youth—the day
dreams of a sensitive student. This unique poem is a poet's
yearning realized as substantial joy. When his course was
nearly run, looking back over his real experiences, he
wished he had seen more of life in his twenties. To pre-
serve his sanity and buoyancy there was only one thing to
cling to: the art of writing.

"The Canadian littérateur," he writes, "must depend
solely upon himself and nature. He is almost without the
exhilaration of lively and frequent literary intercourse . . .
that force and variety of stimulus which counts for so
much in the fructification of ideas." *At the Mermaid Inn*
was a rather sorry attempt to create a centre for the dissemination of ideas. Lampman, I believe, took it very
seriously. He expressed his views on books, on cremation,
on the woman question; one or two of the descriptive[8]
and critical[9] paragraphs are the best he ever wrote. But
that was not what he meant by literary intercourse. Consequently ideas languished and died out. The poet strolled

---

[8]Toronto *Globe*, Feb. 20; Sep. 3; Dec. 24, 1892.
[9]*Ibid.*, Sept. 10, 1892: on Henry James.

off into the country and found complete serenity only
when the city was completely forgotten. Lampman was a
promeneur solitaire not haunted by hallucinations, it is
true, nor yet gifted with the introspective power of Jean-
Jacques. The country was his love, his life, his adventure:
"Just to see and hear." His definition of life is now,

> To lie at length and watch the swallows pass,
> As blithe and restful as this quiet grass.

. . . .

> Blue, blue was the heaven above me,
>   And the earth green at my feet;
> "O Life! O Life!" I kept saying
>   And the very word seemed sweet.

His supreme art was the illustration of nature, the mighty
mother; the glorification of it in finished, beautiful verse;
the slow recitation of its wild flowers, as saints' names in
a litany.[10]

In his earlier mood, and to a certain distance out of the
city, he noticed the country folk at their labours:

> Up the steep slope the horses stamp and strain,
> Urged on by hoarse-tongued drivers—cheeks ablaze.

. . . .

> A little old brown woman on her knees
> Searches the deep hot grass for strawberries.

He listened to the "golden music" of the hermit thrush
and the "five pure notes" of the dreary white-throat. He
recorded his impressions in nicely chosen words:

> The curly horns of ribbed icicles.

. . . .

> warm lucent shadows on the brown
> Leaf-paven pools.

---

[10]*Ibid.*, May 14, 1892.

Later, and farther from the city, he stops, and with deliberate purpose he forces his eye to register the characteristic
details that compose the scene. He must be careful to keep
the precision of the details as he works them up into a
perfect, living picture.

Watch him before the canvas of a sonnet pencilled in
for a sunset. Mountains to the left, hay-carts on the river
beach, the incoming tide and the opposite shore of the
St. Lawrence are there under his eye. Now what happens
to that canvas is the work of Archibald Lampman:

> Broad shadows fall. On all the mountain side
> The scythe-swept fields are silent. Slowly home
> By the long beach the high-piled hay-carts come,
> Splashing the pale salt shallows. Over wide
> Fawn-coloured wastes of mud the slipping tide,
> Round the dun rocks and wattled fisheries,
> Creeps murmuring in. And now by twos and threes,
> O'er the slow spreading pools with clamorous chide,
> Belated crows from strip to strip take flight.
> Soon will the first star shine; yet ere the night
> Reach onward to the pale-green distances,
> The sun's last shaft beyond the gray sea-floor
> Still dreams upon the Kamouraska shore,
> And the long line of golden villages.

As a contrast to this depersonalized landscape, and
impersonal pentameter line, turn to look at it again
through the temperament of his friend, D. C. Scott, who is
there with him. Scott gives us an overdose of feeling by
making us chant a dirge to the tune of "A Psalm of Life":

> Far and faintly far to southward
>   Like an hamlet dim of dreams,
> White the line of Kamouraska
>   In the mirage floats and gleams.[11]

---

[11]"At Murray Bay" in *The Week*, Vol. ix, 1891-2.

How well Lampman has learned the art of the realist! Under his brush all things have become real, have taken the time (the length of a line or so) to exist, have elongated themselves, as they actually do, in the penumbra; the rhymes too: "fisheries," "distances," "villages." The work has been done for its own sake, for the joy of making alive. Yet "silent," "slowly," "dreams," are a poet's words, not a painter's. The work is not absolutely plastic and impassive; an intangible quietness and repose and warmth linger over the lines and colours. Lampman's poems exhale a delicious native aroma, but there is something more, something rarer in his work, something which attracts us to Lampman as a stylist; for he had the artist's nice discernment, a feeling for adjectives and verbs, an ear that hung upon the euphony of a phrase, and, when he cared to use it, a talent, striking at any time, for dissociating commonplaces: ". . . delicate blossoms of arrowhead that seem *made of snowflakes that may melt as you look at them;*" ". . . a few cloud-like flakes of foliage that seem *to have drifted off from its stem and to lie afloat upon the inaccessible air.*" Such phrases are as flashes of warm sunshine bursting through realistic prose.

Lampman did not always maintain a high level of excellence. Often and often he wrote under the stimulus of earlier poets and critics. Often he affected the "poetic" mannerisms of his own and other days, often the spiritual and temporal cant of his time and environment. But he found his natural powers and cultivated them. He was still young when he died. It is not easy to believe that he would have written greater poetry had he lived longer, but he would, assuredly, with the talents at his command, have given us a greater measure of masterly prose, of which he left us far too little.

Young Canadian poets today find no pleasure in Lampman. An art which proceeds directly from a purely sensual apprehension of the exterior world and bears no mystic tokens of having sojourned among the deep-sea fauna of the poet's consciousness cannot stir their minds. Fashions change. The dominant influence in those days was Matthew Arnold's Hellenism; today it is T. S. Eliot's asceticism. When Lampman left the city, his purpose was not to carol forth his heart's sorrow and despair among the mosses and lichens of the tundra, but to contemplate "beauty at its source where the water is clear and flows limpidly with a small, pure stream,"[12] unimpeded by the pebbles of erudite allusions. Despite the irony of his life when contrasted with his sentiments, he was Greek in his art. He described nature in "the faithful way" because he saw things as in themselves they really are.

[12]Toronto *Globe*, Nov. 26, 1892.

AMONG THE MILLET

RALPH GUSTAFSON

It would seem that Canada is about to acquire its "poor Johnny Keats." Archibald Lampman, Professor E. K. Brown has declared, is "our Canadian symbol of the fragile artist worn down by the rigours of our . . . social and economic structure." The picture of the sensitive unfortunate poet succumbing to disregard and the philistinism of his environment is not a new one in literary accounts. Poets are sensitive and their social and economic circumstances have generally been inimical. But the conclusion that they are inwardly defeated by the extraneous is indulgence in romanticism. Lorca succumbed only to a fascist

"Among the Millet," by Ralph Gustafson. In *Northern Review* 1 (February-March 1947), 26-34. By permission of the author.

bullet. Keats was not killed by a quarterly review. Nor—to descend to a minor poetic plane—was Lampman the victim of nefarious Ottawa. To say otherwise is to do injustice to the poet and to mistake the fibre of poetry.

Lampman and his poetry have recently been subjected to much scrutiny. Some of this has been enlightening and well intentioned. Some of it has been prejudiced and sentimental. Lampman's poetry justifies critical attention. "In Canada," as Professor Brown says, "Lampman is the nearest approach to a national classic in verse." Canada has had a thin and intra-mural poetic reputation, and we have consequently been at some extraordinary efforts in our sensitivity on this score to buttress and inflate the good we have produced into a semblance of an aggressive and comparative best. But aside from the literary chauvinism we may have adopted at times in the past, Canada has been right to acclaim its poetry and to protest its neglect, whether at home or abroad. Lampman is not only one of the finest poets which Canada has produced but in a few lyrics and sonnets of nature takes his place with the best in the English language. Recognition of that fact is yet to be achieved.

Meanwhile, however, it would be as well for Canadian criticism to value Lampman for the right reasons. The critical fanfare which has greeted the poem called *At the Long Sault*—recently published for the first time—is, I think, not only exaggerated but another symptom of that harmful malady of Canadian criticism; judging its material by historical significance or "Canadianism" rather than by intrinsic merit. In certain quarters, attempts are evident to claim Lampman for factional reasons, or to cashier him for nonconformity to contemporary pigeon-holes. Thus, their "unexpected social awareness" leads Mr. Irving Layton, in *First Statement*, to highlight Lampman's *Epitaph on a Rich Man* and *Liberty*—two very mediocre poems indeed. On the other hand, Mr. John Sutherland, in *Direction,* would throw out the baby with the bath-water: "Lampman expended more energy," he complains, "in getting away from Ottawa and its citizens than in any other form of practical endeavour." Mr. Patrick Anderson, in *En Masse,* inadequately defines Lampman as seeing himself as "the subjective ego lost in the wilderness."

Amidst this contemporary critical sentimentalization, exaggeration and grinding of axes, where is the true Lampman and his poetry? The crux of the Lampman matter is the relation between the poet and the Ottawa at the end of the last century, as these critics indicate. But was Lampman "situated hopelessly on the outskirts of civilization"? Was his poetic nature stultified by being forced to work in a city which he describes as "utterly destitute of all light and charm"? Was Lampman poetically frustrated because Ottawa was at that time the scene of political corruption? Did such circumstances heighten Lampman's association with nature? Or did he decamp and avoid facing life? If he was not a social poet, should he have been?

The answers to such questions are, of course, the business of criticism only in so far as they elucidate Lampman's literary position. The knowledge that Ottawa girded Lampman into writing *The City of the End of Things* won't make the piece a good poem. The historical understanding of why a poet didn't write what he couldn't won't increase his stature. The perspective of two generations later has little interest in historical complaints or the excuses of environment. That is as it should be. Poetry is of worth, not in spite of, only because of.

But Lampman was profoundly affected in his writing by his circumstances and the understanding of these is necessary to the full understanding of the poetry. As Professor W. E. Collin points out: "If the deepest and most secret elements of Lampman's nature were involved in his poetry it seems reasonably certain that we can understand neither without the other."

What those elements were it is, of course, impossible to define completely. At some point one must conjecture even with the most self-revelatory of poets. And Lampman was not given to personal revelation in his poetry. That there was some great emotional crisis in the life of Lampman is evident. His friend and biographer, Duncan Campbell Scott, sensed "the existence but not the plot of an intense personal drama." And despite the fact that, in another place, Scott characterizes Lampman as "without perplexity or inward brooding," there is abundant evidence in the poems of a profound and lasting inward drama:

> As one sick and blind,
> Round and still round an old and fruitless theme,
> I toiled, nor saw the golden morning light,
> Nor heard the sparrows singing, but the sweat
> Beaded my brow and made my pillow wet.
> So seared and withered as a plant with blight,
> Eaten by passion, stripped of all my pride,
> I wished that somehow then I might have died.
>
> (*Sorrow*)

(Such sorrow can hardly be confined to the death in 1894 of a son who lived only a few months—a subject which Lampman treated in another sonnet of much less moving power.) To such a crisis we have no specific clue.

The cast of Lampman's nature seems from the first to have been toward melancholy. Life, Lampman says in a sonnet, *Despondency*, in his first book, seems

> Vain and phantasmal as a sick man's dream.

He was precipitated at times into hypochondria. During the period of his best poems he wrote: "I am getting well weary of things. I was so far gone in hypochondria on Saturday last that I had not the spirit to go to my office at all." In one of his later sonnets, *Death*, he says: "I like to stretch full-length upon my bed," imagine the body a corpse and the inquiries into

> What spirit, or what fire, could ever have been
> Within that yellow and discoloured mask.

At the same time, there can be no doubt about Lampman's happiness in the very fact of being alive. The ultimate explanation probably lies simply in that awareness of *Lacrimae rerum*, the passage of time and the transience of beauty, which have affected all poets. It is probable that Lampman could not have given us the answer:

> With all dear things that ought to please
> The hours are blessed,
> And yet my soul is ill at ease
> And cannot rest.
> (*Unrest*)

In *Winter-Store*, he says:

> through the night,
> Comes a passion and a cry,
> With a blind sorrow and a might,
> I know not whence, I know not why,
> A something I cannot control,
> A nameless hunger of the soul.

Lampman, at once, found life "strangely sad" (*Music*) and himself "strangely happy" (*The Sweetness of Life*). It is the human paradox.

From such sensitive unrest derives much of the essential appeal of Lampman's poetry. It has given his best sonnets their valid profundity. The question of Ottawa and Lampman's specific circumstances is a further matter, and one which did not have such happy results for his poetry.

Lampman sustained his writing as a civil servant in the Post Office Department at Ottawa from 1883 until the

close of the century. In prose, Lampman exclaimed: "It is
freedom that I want. I am bound. I am suffocated. If I
had the genius of Milton I could do nothing." In poetry,
he cried out:

> The city smites me with its dissonant roar.
> (*April*)

He found little in Ottawa but "Rude fates, hard hearts,
and prisoning poverty" (*A Night of Storm*). It would be
insensitive to minimize "the shallow toil, the strife against
the grain" (*April*) which was the lot of Lampman, and yet
in examining the numerous denunciations and rejections
of Ottawa and the men in it to be found in his poetry, the
suspicion cannot be avoided that Lampman protested too
much and in too general terms. The conclusion is forced
upon one that Lampman was shifting responsibility from
himself, that his protests were compensation for a lack
that lay elsewhere than wholly in his environment. Lampman's attitude is one of over-simplification and melodrama. With all due consideration of his health, his isolation from cultured society, his routine and economic
struggle, our artist was not so fragile that he was worn out
by the harshness of Ottawa's social structure.

It is the present contention that Ottawa gave impetus to
the natural trend of his talent; that his situation con-
ributed to his personal, lyric association with nature. The
essence of Lampman's nature was one with the Romantic
Revival, the Return to Nature. Ottawa was further instiga-
tion to seek what he truly desired to have; its iniquities,
a dramatic justification of his beliefs. The "uncivilized"
landscape of Ontario provided him with the material
without which he would have been poetically bankrupt.
It would not have been better if life had set him down in
literary London. Lampman did not face "life" in Ontario.
The facts are contrary to Professor Collin's conclusion that
Lampman was "cheated out of life," that the respectability

of Ottawa stifled him. We have Duncan Campbell Scott's
word for it that Lampman "never worked in loneliness or
without appreciation." (It is a pertinent fact that the poet
Scott himself lived in Lampman's Ottawa.) As for respectability, are there not indications that Lampman partook
willingly of puritan provincialism—the pinning down of
the pages in his manuscript containing the unexceptional
love sonnets; his judgment of the "brawny passion" of
Charles Robert's *In Notre Dame*; his poem of how *Abu
Midjan* renounced forever the bottle?

Lampman, at too great a cost to his natural endowments, clung too hard to a literal interpretation of Matthew Arnold's postulation that "poetry is a criticism of
life," to his own belief that "the greatest poets, those few
who are eminent above all others for dignity and majesty
of tone, have been men of affairs before they were poets."
The quality which Lampman admired in the poetry of
his contemporary fellow-countryman, George Frederick
Cameron, was that the thought is "always sharp from the
battle of life." Lampman felt it his own poetic duty to
throw himself into "the battle of life." Yet had he done so
would he not still have yearned to find himself where
"the battle of life shall cease" (*Freedom*)—in all proba-
bility have ultimately found himself "far up in the wild
and wintry hills in the heart of the cliff-broken woods"
(*The Woodcutter's Hut*), at least poetically? One need
not take too literally Scott's statement that the only existence Lampman coveted was "that of a bushman to be
constantly hidden in the heart of the woods," but the
poems fully support Scott's observation that Lampman
"disliked exercising his practical endowments."

This confusion of purpose and personality persisted
throughout Lampman's short life (is perhaps an illustration of the principle which Yeats propounds, of a man
desiring his opposite). The belief that it was a poetic duty
to throw one's self into the traffic of life was no less real

for being an intellectual assumption on the part of Lampman. But his natural temperament rebelled at every opportunity. It is the key to the poems.

To be a "man of affairs" was a possibility (as far as Lampman's health would permit) even in the Ottawa of the eighteen-nineties. Lampman could have faced the issue; and by failure or success resolved it. Lampman turned his back on it; but he never forgot.

The memory did not serve his poetry well. His poems of social observation no longer come alive for the simple reason that they were not vital to Lampman—though he thought they were. His assumed aspiration for "life" proved not only intolerable as a self-discipline but recalcitrant as poetic material.

> [The poet] must walk with men that reel
> On the rugged path, and feel
> Every sacred soul that is
> Beating very near to his.
> Simple, human, careless, free,
> As God made him, he must be.
> (*What Do Poets Want with Gold*)

The self-appointed "rugged path" and yet the instinctive "careless"!

Another aspect of the contradiction is revealed in *At the Ferry*. It is a poem conveying in some nine stanzas of distinctive concrete power the Canadian scene:

> On such a day at every rod
> The toilers in the hayfield halt,
> With dripping brows, and the parched sod
> Yields to the crushing foot like salt.

The stanzas are alive with life. Lampman need not have denied it—even though Ottawa could not substitute for "peopled hills, and ancient fields / And cities by the crested sea":

> I see no more the barges pass,
>   Nor mark the ripple round the pier,
> And all the uproar, mass on mass,
>   Falls dead upon a vacant ear.
> Beyond the tumult of the mills,
>   And all the city's sound and strife.
> Beyond the waste, beyond the hills,
>   I look far out and dream of life.

It is unconscionable.

Lampman's inability to fulfill the worldly role he thought he should assume led him to postulations that the world was well lost. "I shall no longer care," he wrote, "whether people pay attention to me or not, whether those I love return my affection or not." His own incapacity must be rationalized into a virtue before it would let him rest. It was necessary that Ottawa be nothing but iniquity, its citizens, "a dim-hearted earthly race / Who creep firm-nailed upon the earth's hard face" (*Aspiration*).

> Nay, for they are not of thy kind,
>   But in a rarer clay
> God dowered thee with an alien mind;
>   Thou canst not be as they.
>   (*To the Prophetic Soul*)

The Cup of Life "turns the half to swine." A remarkable attitude for the sonneteer of Chaucer! The poetry took on the quality of purple spotlights and hissings of villains:

> The curses of gold are about thee . . . .
>
> . . . .
>
> And the guest-hall boometh and shrilleth,
>   With the dance's mocking sound.

. . . .

In chambers of gold elysian,
    The cymbals clash and clang . . . .
                    (*The City*)

Out of the heat of the usurer's hold,
    From the horrible crash of the strong man's feet;
Out of the shadow where pity is dying;
Out of the clamour where beauty is lying,
Dead in the depth of the struggle for gold;
    Out of the din and the glare of the street . . . .
                    (*Freedom*)

A melodrama fatal to much of his poetry. The conflict might have held a masterpiece. But that was not for Lampman.

It has been maintained that Lampman in his last years was increasingly tending toward "the drama of life." Professor Brown particularly cites as evidence the poem about Daulac and his heroic stand *At the Long Sault*. One would be more willing to accept the theory if the poem had been about the drama of life contemporary to Lampman. However that may be, the main point is the poetry, and here one cannot agree that *At the Long Sault* bears out the prophecy that Lampman would have written poems of "the drama of life" that could have been set beside the earlier splendid nature pieces. The vaunted passage likening Daulac's stand to

                a tired bull-moose
    Whom scores of sleepless wolves, a ravening pack,
    Have chased all night, all day,

is really an evasion.

Lampman, then, having argued that the world was well lost, intensified a mode of thought that would at once be compensation and justification. Abstractions were allowed to substitute for experience. Capitalized Beauty, Love, Truth, Justice, Eternity, stuff his lines—good poetic currency when each has an exact referant in the context, but words which offer a too tempting escape from thinking

and accuracy of imagination. Poetry is the species before
the genus. The reality of Platonic abstractions, Descartes'
veritates aeternae, are not conveyed by naming them.
Lampman in this was, of course, using the poetic stock in
trade contemporary to him, but, with him, it too often
became the poetic line of least resistance. He becomes
meaningless. He implores us, for example, to be

> Something radiant and august as night,
> Something wide as space . . . .
> *(Alcyone)*

Elation, yes; but verse "where no faintest gust of life comes
ever" (ibid.). He adjures us to "breathe once more the
wind of the Eternal . . . at rest upon the cool infinitude
of Space and Time" (*An Ode to the Hills*). This is negation of life: it is the negation of the artist—who by the
particular proves the eternal.

Lampman, finally, sought further justification in an
exaltation of "reverie." But Reverie was made synony-
mous with "thinking"; "dreaming" was used to detour
experience. Professor Brown, in his excellent book, *On
Canadian Poetry,* argues that when Lampman "dreams"
he "feels the essence of the scene in which he finds himself." The truth is that it is at those points where Lampman dreams that the poet fails to penetrate his experience.
Duncan Campbell Scott points out that Lampman and
Wordsworth "were as one in speaking of nature as a
refuge, but the greater poet used the shelter to recreate
his interest in life, and not as a nook for reverie."

Fortunately, at times, what Lampman meant by "dreaming" was intense penetration of concrete experience. Fortunately, in the words of Yeats, "we make out of the
quarrel with ourselves, poetry." Through all his personal
confusion and justification, in a dozen poems Lampman
came directly into passionate contact with nature, made
concentric the observed and the observer, and wrote it
down in memorable language. Beyond the city gates,

Lampman's whole being became vitalized. The Canadian landscape became a joy almost painfully extreme to Lampman's sensitive spirit:

> Blue, blue was the heaven above me,
> And the earth green at my feet;
> "O Life! O Life!" I kept saying,
> And the very word seemed sweet.
> (*Life and Nature*)

For all his "cosmic consciousness" he did not forget to observe:

> The curly horns of ribbed icicles
> (*Winter*)

> The far-off hayfields where the dusty teams
> Drive round and round the lessening squares of hay.
> (*Comfort of the Fields*)

> soon from height to height,
> With silence and the sharp unpitying stars,
> Stern creeping frosts, and winds that touch like steel,
> Out of the depth beyond the eastern bars,
> Glittering and still shall come the awful night.
> (*Winter Evening*)

> By others let great epics be compiled;
> For me, the dreamer, 'tis enough to know
> The lyric stress, the fervour sweet and wild:
> I sit me in the windy grass and grow
> As wise as age, as joyous as a child.
> (*Ambition*)

Lampman once declared: "I do not care a hang for anything but poetry." He achieved it in a dozen pieces. It is not much, as the product of great poets goes. But the quality of his little is of the best. It alone serves as retort beautiful to such statements as that of the English poet, Louis MacNeice, who regretfully informed the People's Forum in Montreal that the Canadian countryside had not been "put on paper in verse."

COPY OF LETTER BY
DUNCAN CAMPBELL SCOTT
TO RALPH GUSTAFSON

17 July '45

Dear Mr. Gustafson:

I have to thank you for your letter of the 13th May and the copy of your article on Lampman. I might have replied sooner but I have been unwell and indisposed to do any work, so my reply has been delayed. Many thanks for your reference to my contributions to your Anthology, I approved them at the time; the book was well received here and I hope you have been gratified with a large circulation. I trust you are active in production and find a ready outlet for what you write.

I wish you might have found a different opening for your article. The phrase "poor Johnny Keats" is not yours, but it should be forgotten. I have not read any late estimates of Lampman but I am familiar with Professor Brown's work and I do not find in his sympathetic treatment of the man, his poems and prose, taken altogether as it should be, any intention to make of the poet a martyr to our social system or to his personal surroundings. You ask me to "comment" on your article. I don't know where the line is to be drawn between criticism and comment but my remarks are to be taken as interested "comment," if at any time they verge on *criticism* you will make due allowance.

I feel that I have said all that I have to say about Lampman and probably the most important remark I have to make about your article is that I am happy to know that you men of this time find his work so worthy of study and

Copy of letter to Ralph Gustafson by Duncan Campbell Scott. In *The Fiddlehead* 41 (Summer 1959), 12-14. By permission of the Estate of Duncan Campbell Scott.

discussion and differences of valuation and misunderstandings which are bound to arise. I think that to fix Ottawa and its society as the *only* source of his outlook on life in the world is a great mistake. I do not think it is Professor Brown's basic feeling about Lampman; I do not extract it from his essays, and do not recollect it from our conversations, Lampman's *mind* cannot be imprisoned in Ottawa it was free to range and did range over World society and events and he was well versed in what went on beyond our boundaries. It ought to be remembered that when he came to Ottawa it was a town of about 23,000 people, and when he died the population had struggled up to say 50,000. There was comparatively no wealth here, there were no strong men here with crashing feet, and there was no din and glare in the streets; a horse-drawn street-car crawled across the girth of the town; we walked about unless we could afford a cab. So that his idea of the cruel world and its society, came to him from the experiences of others, from his socialistic proclivities; he was a confirmed socialist of the Fabian type, the only coherent association anywhere in the English-speaking world. This experience and its forthcoming ideas were suffered by him and used as a foil against his vision of the world as he would remake it.

I think I should make a note here on the Nature that most affected L. In my Memoir I wrote about his removal to Ottawa; "He was on the borders of the wild nature that he loved." When I wrote an article for Dr. Percival of the Education Department of Quebec I made a special reference to the influence that Quebec scenery had upon him. I introduced Lampman to the immediate north lands of the Gatineau and the Lièvre and to camping and canoeing, a sort of life that he had never known, and to the Lower St Lawrence. This scenery with its romantic appeal had a great effect upon his nature work; such fine poems as "Between the Rapids," "Morning on the Lièvre," "Sunset at Les Eboulements," "A Dawn on the Lièvre," "In the

Wilds," and many others. And the experience of a new kind of freedom with scope for his virility and prowess on making use of his muscles was of great value to him.

In writing that "coveted" the life of a bushman I wrote a sentence that is exaggerated and may be readily misinterpreted; I gave it as a too careless opinion. In my opinion it may be classed with Professor Brown's remark that Ottawa "Almost corrupted Lampman"; although I have never mentioned the point to him. When Lampman speaks for himself he looks forward to superannuation and a home in some quiet country place where he can give himself up to Poetry. On p. 29 of your article you quote the sentence, "If I had the genius of Milton I could do nothing." The wish to co-ordinate his work should, I think, have led you to quote what went before as to his modest hopes for the future. The exclamation about Milton arose, no doubt, from extreme irritation; possibly no more than some office restriction or "fault-finding." His calm outlook on the future is more characteristic. The bondage that he disliked was office routine. There were all sorts of annoyances in the Service. When he entered it the hours were from half-after-nine to four in the afternoon and the clerks had to bring their lunches and eat them in the office. After 1896 the conditions rather worsened. All statutory increases were stopped by the Liberal Government and were not renewed until after Lampman's death and he with all others were deprived of what they had a right to expect.

Lampman never wanted to be a man of affairs or felt sense at failure to be such. Actually he took a keen interest in human psychology and conduct. Some of his best poems deal with mind and possibilities of man such as "The Largest Life," "Stoic and Hedonist," etc. He was interested in both life and nature and there was no "confusion" or "contradiction" in this. As an artist he excelled in nature work in which he had few peers; he wrote well of "life" too but no better than many others; therefore, his high place in our letters is reared on his nature poems rather than on those dealing with human affairs.

Your idea that Ottawa "grided" Lampman into writing "The City of the End of Things" is quite erroneous, and reading it after a long lapse I know what a fine thing it is. This poem had no possible source in Ottawa past or present. It was not a reaction to Ottawa in any way. It was "builded in the leafless tracts and valleys huge of Tartarus" suggestive of the cities we are now told will have to be built underground in the atomic age. You should read this poem again and get the cosmic and dynamic effect of it, the clash and clang and roar of the machine age grinding itself to death and ending in imbecility and silence. This poem is a prophecy and warning; strange that it was written in the quietudes of the 90s when it so graphically portrays the atmosphere of a half a century later and the very fears that lurk in thinking men's minds in the second post world war era. And how could Ottawa produce the three noble sonnets on Crete that Professor Brown and I published for the first time in "At the Long Sault"? No further evidence beyond these sonnets, written with all his skill in this form as late as October 1896, is needed to show his interest in World events and his indignation at cruelty and injustice.

The cast of Lampman's nature was not towards melancholy. Like most brilliant men he had his emotional storms and variations of mood, and he had to contend with bad health which depresses anybody. He had a great sense of humor and was a man of geniality and sociability. . . . I cannot agree that Lampman was "cheated out of life"; that phrase is not appropriate to a man whose life was so full of endeavour and accomplishment. . . .

What the future held for him who can predict? All speculation is idle but one will indulge it. He was thirty-eight when he died not worn out by a conflict with Ottawa and its parochial society, but from a gradual heart-weakening and a final burst of exertion too great. But for myself

I believe in the possibility of greater achievement because
I know the real strength of his spirit and mind, his venera-
tion for great poetry and his resolute contemplation of
"life" as it developed in his time. When a man reaches
the age of thirty-eight he may be just on the threshold of
his fame.

I have already written at too great length but it will
give you to understand that I value your article. This
letter is for yourself alone, I have done with writing for
the public about this great Poet of ours.

I have been reading again those poems of yours available to me in the Anthologies; your own, Mr Dilworth's,
and Mr Smith's. I always get much pleasure in reading
"Dedication" and that is what I ever read poetry for, and
I am glad that Mr Smith put "Epithalamium in Time of
War" into his collection; a poem that is full of feeling,
and I am glad to enjoy it without trying to "co-ordinate"
it with a personality.

With many thanks for your good letter and for your
essay in *The Northern Review* in which I was constantly
interested and with cordial regards,

> I am
> > yours sincerely,
> > > (signed) DUNCAN C. SCOTT

EDGAR ALLAN POE IN CANADA

JOHN SUTHERLAND

It appears to me that . . . he has told us what he had to tell us in his own way, that he has escaped from his early masters.
                                    E. K. Brown on Archibald Lampman.

Edgar Allan Poe always said that the climax of his tour of Canada, when he lectured at Cameron Heights, MacInnesville, Carmanopolis, and other centres, came with his visit to Ottawa and Archibald Lampman. Poe was as fond of pranks as a schoolboy, and a freakish incident occurred on his arrival at Ottawa station. Professor E. K. Brown, the author of *On Canadian Poetry*, who headed the welcoming delegation (the ailing Lampman was confined to his home), was told that Poe's password would be "nevermore," that he would use the alias, "Israfel," and that, in case of a slip-up, he could always be recognized by his habit of reciting his own poetry while perched on a bust of Pallas. Of course, Poe switched to "rapid Pleiad" and introduced himself as "Alcyone." Brown, who had previously welcomed Keats, Wordsworth, Arnold and Tennyson on Lampman's behalf, and had always penetrated their disguises, failed to recognize the American genius. He was completely mystified when Poe got up on Pallas and began reciting *Alcyone*, a copy of which Lampman had recently sent him with a request for his comment:

> In the silent depth of space,
> Immeasurably old, immeasurably far,
> Glittering with a silver flame
> Through eternity,

"Edgar Allan Poe in Canada," by John Sutherland. In *Northern Review* 4 (February-March 1951), 22-37. By permission of the Estate of John Sutherland.

> Rolls a great and burning star,
> With a noble name,
>   Alcyone!
> In the glorious chart of heaven
> It is marked the first of seven;
> 'Tis a Pleiad . . . .
>
>   (*Alcyone*)

Apparently still unaware that the stranger was Poe, Brown makes this irrelevant comment on p. 115 of *On Canadian Poetry:* "The blend of rhyming and unrhyming lines, long lines and short lines, in an irregular pattern, is one of Lampman's experiments." It should have been obvious that the opening lines of *Alcyone* were only a veiled transcription of Poe's *Israfel*:

> In heaven a spirit doth dwell
> "Whose heart strings are a lute";
> None sing so wildly well
> As the angel Israfel,
> And the giddy stars (so legends tell)
> Ceasing their hymns, attend the spell
>   Of his voice, all mute . . . .
>
> While, to listen, the red levin,
> (With the rapid Pleiads, even,
> Which were seven)
> Pauses in Heaven.
>
>   (*Israfel*)

Just examine the two passages together and keep a general picture of Poe in your mind. The Pleiads in *Alcyone* (the title poem of Lampman's last book) are a direct link with *Israfel*, an unmistakable clue, and the rest of the poem is very easily decoded. The "noble name" echoes the lordly "name" of *The Raven*: Poe was almost obsessed with the word "name," partly because it agreed with his ideas of aristocratic grandeur, and partly because he regarded grandeur, like beauty, as essentially corrupt, and identified "name" with "stigma." "Alcyone" itself, with its mythic associations, is a patent substitute for "Israfel": "Israfel," it is true, is described as a spirit with the gift of song and not as a star; yet in the first stanza of *Israfel*, the stars are said to be "ceasing their hymns," and at the end of *Alcyone* Lampman speaks of "the music of its name"—meaning his star. Nearly every important word in the Lampman passage—"silent," "space," "old," "far," "flame," "burning" and "rolls"—is common in Poe's vocabulary. Brown's incomprehension is, therefore, difficult to understand. So far as its form is concerned, *Alcyone* is obviously based on the extremely varied stanzas of *Israfel*, and the free positioning of the rime, though not the riming pattern, is from the same model.

Or at least this is true of the form of the passage above, the opening lines of the poem. In the next lines the *Israfel* pattern is abandoned in favour of a meter which Poe uses in *Dream-Land* and in other poems:

> It has *travelled* all that time—
> Thought has not a swifter flight—
> Through a *region* where no faintest gust
> Of life comes ever, but *the power of night*
> Dwells stupendous and *sublime,*
> Limitless and void and *lonely,*
> A *region* mute with age, and peopled *only*
> With the dead and ruined dust
> Of worlds that lived eternities ago.
> (Alcyone)

> By a route obscure and *lonely,*
> Haunted by ill angels *only,*
> Where *an Eidolon, named Night,*
> On a black throne reigns upright,
> I have reached these lands but newly
> From an ultimate dim Thule—
> From a wild weird clime that lieth, *sublime,*
> Out of SPACE—out of TIME . . .

> For the heart whose woes are legion
> 'Tis a peaceful, soothing *region* . . .
> But the *traveller, travelling* through it,
> May not—dare not openly view it . . .
>   (*Dream-Land*)

My underlinings [italics] tell their own story. If anything, the imitative note is more pronounced than in the opening passage.

The result of this change of form is to throw *Alcyone* completely out of joint. Unfortunately, that is not the end of the matter. Just at this point the poem suffers a sea-change, and we hear the voice of the merman, Matthew Arnold:

> Man! when thou dost think of this,
> And what our earth and its existence is,
> The half-blind toils since life began,
> The little aims, the little span,
> With what passion and what pride,
> And what hunger fierce and wide,
> Thou dost break beyond it all,
> Seeking for the spirit unconfined
> In the clear abyss of mind
> A shelter and a peace majestical.

Insofar as these lines continue the trochaic couplets of Dream-Land, they still contain rhythmic echoes of Poe: insofar as they express a discontent with the "half-blind toils" of material existence, and a yearning to "break beyond it all" into "a peace majestical," they echo the exalted didactic tone of Arnold. Even this is not the end of Lampman's gymnastics: in the last lines of *Alcyone* he takes another whirl on the bars with Israfel!

We will find Poe's influence in much of the later Lampman, especially where he grows preoccupied with death or the supernatural, but there are four other poems in which it is present in a most direct and imitative way: *War, A Vision of Twilight, The Vase of Ibn Mokbil* and *The City of the End of Things* (a poem I will discuss in detail later on). *War* is most reminiscent of *The Haunted Palace* and *The Conqueror Worm*—in the feverish pace of the rhythm, the feminine riming (often drawn from exotic place names), and the rich clusters of consonants:

> I can hear the horn of Uri
>   Roaring in the hills enorm;
> Kindled at its brazen fury,
>   I can see the clansmen form;
> In the dawn in misty masses,
> Pouring from the silent passes
> Over Granson or Morgarten
>   Like the storm.

A Vision of Twilight, a poem rather similar in technique, is thick with verbal echoes of Poe[1] (I have italicized some of the more obvious):

> By a *void* and soundless river
>   On the outer edge of space,
> Where the body comes not ever,
>   But the absent dream hath place,
> Stands a city tall and quiet,
>   And its air is sweet and dim;
> Never sound of grief or riot
>   Makes it mad, or makes it *grim*.
>
> And the tender skies thereover
>   Neither sun, nor star, behold—
> Only dusk it hath for cover,—
>   But a glamour soft with gold,

---

[1] There are also occasional echoes of Swinburne's *The Garden of Prosperine*. The influence of Swinburne may be traced elsewhere—for example, in *Freedom* in the early book, *Among the Millet*:

> Out of the heart of the city begotten
> Of the labour of men and their manifold hands
> Whose souls, that were sprung from the earth in the morning,
> No longer regard or remember her warning, etc.

Through a mist of dreamier *essence*
  Than the dew of twilight, smiles
On strange shafts and domes and *crescents*,
  Lifting into *eerie* piles.

In its courts and hallowed places
  Dreams of distant worlds arise,
Shadows of transfigured faces,
  Glimpses of immortal eyes,
Echoes of serenest pleasure,
  Notes of perfect speech that fall,
Through an air of endless leisure,
  Marvellously musical . . . .[1]
Wandering by that gray and solemn
  Water, with its *ghostly* quays—
Vistas of *vast* arch and column,
  Shadowed by unearthly trees—
Biddings of sweet power compel me . . . .

The Vase of Ibn Mokbil is also imitative of Poe's rhythms
and sometimes of his language:

Full of woe was Ibn Mokbil
    To behold
      Brothers overtaken
By misfortune—*sitting restless
In his house forlorn and guestless,*
      With a larder
Empty, and a purse forsaken
    Of its gold . . .
To the ears of Ibn Mokbil
    Angels tell
      Tales of how the bringer

---

[1]Cf. this stanza with *The Haunted Palace*:
    Wanderers in that happy valley,
      Through two luminous windows, saw
    Spirits moving musically
      To a lute's well-tuned law . . .
    A troop of Echoes, whose sweet duty
      Was but to sing,
    In voices of surpassing beauty,
      The wit and wisdom of their king . . .

> Of the old faith still careth
> For the foot that strictly fareth.
>> As he listens,
> Falls *a voice divine, the singer,*
>> *Israfel.*

None of Lampman's early poems is reminiscent of Poe, with the exception of *Easter Eve* in *Among the Millet*. Here, again, the riming has the special Poe twist (e.g., "eerie," "weary," "miserere"), and there are various lines and passages which suggest both *Ulalume* and *The Haunted Palace*. Poe's poetic trademark, "no more" ("nevermore" in The Raven, for the sake of the alliterative "v") also comes into play:

> They remember now no more

> On the silence fell no more

> And the revel rose no more

> Swooning, and I knew no more

It is worth noting that the first stanzas of *Easter Eve* are imitative of Coleridge's *The Ancient Mariner*—a poem which had an influence on Poe's own work.

The phenomenon I mentioned above—the conjuncture of Arnold and Poe—is present to some degree in all these poems. It is a strange combination, explicable only in terms of Lampman's misconception of poetry and his inherent mistrust of his art. He regarded poetry as an escape into dream, a kind of opiate, but he never ceased to feel that the desire to escape was slightly corrupt. Hence, as in *Alcyone*, he always felt obliged to relate the hazy reaches of the dream to a large moral truth, no matter how incongruous it might seem. What was, in effect, a split between the imagination and reality grew steadily wider. In the early poems Keats and Wordsworth were the two opposing influences: in the main Keats stood for the doves of the dream, Wordsworth for the pillars of reality. The split was underlined by the gradual change to the Arnold-Poe combination (with Tennyson sometimes substituting for Poe). Arnold supplanted Wordsworth as moral mentor, but Arnold could only teach Lampman the need for clinging grimly to the fragments of a dissolving world, or the possible dawn of a new one, without offering any clear purpose or plan of positive action. Although the influence of Keats still lingers on the later poems, Poe (and Tennyson) had largely supplanted Keats, and Poe more than anyone could satisfy that thirst for escape which Lampman felt more and more. The dislocations which occur in some of the early poems, where the Wordsworth influence conflicts with that of Keats, are even more marked in the later poetry, especially where the influences of Poe and Arnold come together. It seems probable that Lampman's illness, which led to his death in 1899, and which may have been latent for several years before it appeared in 1896, accounts for the flagging energy, the loss of sharpness and clarity, and the growing morbidity of his later work, and explains the attraction he felt for Poe.

In discussing Poe's influence above, I used the word "imitative" on several occasions. Before continuing with the last of the Poe poems, *The City of the End of Things*, perhaps I should explain just how I interpret both "imitative" and "individual." In the first place, I assume the obvious fact that an imitative and an individual element may often be found in the same poem or the same poet. Let me illustrate the point with an example from Lampman's early work: the well-known *Heat*, a poem often praised by Lampman's critics and perhaps his nearest approach to a genuinely personal expression. *Heat* is a curious poem—curious in the sense that it manages to suggest the cold emptiness of the north even while it vividly re-creates the summer landscape:

> This wagon on the height above,
>   From sky to sky on either hand,
> Is the sole thing that seems to move
>   In all the heat-held land.

Knowing Lampman, I don't think we can read that line, "From sky to sky on either hand," with its effect of blind vacancy, and not be reminded of other poems in which he describes the Canadian landscape as a place of terrifying desolation—perhaps of that passage in *The City of the End of Things* where the "bulk that never moves a jot" "Sits looking toward the lightless north." He "leans at rest and drains the heat"—stretching his hands out to the blaze of summer but feeling the "lightless north" like a cold room at his back. To my mind, it is this paradoxical element which makes *Heat* a more intense, and more nearly individual poem, than anything else in Lampman: the balance between the two contrasting moods—between the self-absorbed content and the intimation of fear—saves him both from the melodramatic effects of his winter landscapes, and—up to a point—from the vagueness of his summer reveries. Yet even here an imitative note obtrudes—especially at the climactic point of the poem, in the lines I have italicized below:

> Where the far elm-tree shadows flood
>   Dark patches in the burning grass,
> The cows, each with her peaceful cud,
>   Lie waiting for the heat to pass.
> *From somewhere on the slope near by*
>   *Into the pale depth of the noon*
> *A wandering thrush slides leisurely*
>   *His thin revolving tune.*

The lines are imitative of Keats—though less in the verbal sense of other seasonal poems, with their direct echoes of the *Ode to a Nightingale* and the ode *To Autumn*, than in the faithful duplication of an aspect of the Keatsian sensibility. There are many passages in Keats that have a similar quality—that subside into a sensuous swoon rendered the more delightful by the little prickings of pain and loss. Lampman, of course, does not have the intensity, or the power of phrase, of Keats at his best. His role here is the familiar one of the imitator, who seizes on that aspect of another sensibility which he can best understand, achieving something of the beauty of the original but also revealing where its excesses lie. His lines are not unmoving, nor lacking in descriptive skill, but they are a bit lush and over-sweet, without the health and sanity of the mature Keats.

I assume, then, that an individual and an imitative quality may often go hand in hand, as they do in *Heat*: I also assume that a fully personal style is not important in its own right. It is not the test of a successful poem, but one of the essential ingredients. Some writers achieve a very distinctive note, without any comparable poetic achievement: Poe himself is the perfect example, for in spite of his great influence and his personal fascination, he is no more than a dexterous sleight-of-hand artist.[1] On the other hand, most Canadian poets suffer from a lack of genuine individuality, and from a parasitic dependence on the literature of other countries. Among the nature poets, it is obvious that the most widely-known—Carman, Roberts and Lampman himself—depend on a periodic saturation in the work of other writers. To read one of them through is like reading an anthology of romantic poetry in English in the nineteenth century—arranged in a loose yet quite suggestive chronological order. It is true that they are not generally guilty of the more obvious imitations of an early poet such as Charles Sangster, but we must not con-

---

[1] Poe was more nearly right than his critics. While we should take his modesty with a grain of salt, he wrote in the preface to his collected poems: "In defence of my own taste . . . it is incumbent upon me to say that I think nothing in this volume of much value to the public, or very creditable to myself".

clude that they have ceased to be imitative and colonial. If we overlook the imitative side of their work, and dress them up with the label "cosmopolitan," we cater to the persistent colonialism of Canadian poetry and Canadian criticism. This mistake was made by the critic, Claude Bissell, in an interesting article, *Literary Taste in Central Canada,* recently published in *The Canadian Historical Review.*

The above remarks apply particularly well to Lampman's *The City of the End of Things,* a poem showing the influence of Poe, highly rated by Canadian critics and anthologists and worthy of detailed discussion. It contains many echoes of *Dream-Land* and *The Haunted Palace,* but, as the title suggests, it is closest to *The City in the Sea.*[1] *The City in the Sea* (the city of death), though often reminiscent of Coleridge's *Kubla Khan,* and especially of parts of Byron's *The Castle of Chillon,* is unmistakably Poe's own work and fully characteristic of his later period. It is still a poor poem, and it is vulgar in the way that only Poe can be vulgar. Very nearly the reverse is true of *The City of the End of Things.* It is one of Lampman's better poems, and it has considerable power and skill. Occasionally, as in the lines I have italicized below, it strikes an original and thoroughly convincing note:

> And at the city gate a fourth,
> Gigantic and with dreadful eyes,
> Sits looking towards the lightless north,
> Beyond the reach of memories;
> *Fast rooted to the lurid floor,*
> *A bulk that never moves a jot,*
> In his pale body dwells no more,
> In mind or soul,—an idiot.

---

[1] Its phrasing is also frequently reminiscent of James Thomson's *The City of Dreadful Night,* as Professor Collin suggests in his essay in *The White Savannahs.* There is, however, the essential difference that, while Lampman (and Poe) try to induce horror by the power of suggestion, Thomson's method is one of careful delineation.

Notice that Lampman speaks here of the "lightless north":
the original note derives from the vivid and concrete
realization of an image of fear—a remark that might be
made of other passages in Lampman and of the work of
other Canadian poets. The passage is reminiscent of the
lines in *The Cachalot* where Pratt describes the bulk of
the kraken rooted to the ocean floor: ·

> Moveless, he seemed, as a boulder set
> In pitch, and dead within his lair,
> Except for a transfixing stare
> From lidless eyes of burnished jet.

Pratt's lines, however, are superior to Lampman's, more
intense and vivid, free both of his lapses of taste (such as
the rime of "jot" and "idiot," a touch of Poe's vulgarity)
and of the derivativeness of phrases like "dreadful eyes"
and "pale body." It is this derivativeness that deprives
The City of the End of Things of its full impact and gives
it the air of a tour-de-force in the Poe manner. Its heavily-
rimed tetrameters (*abab*) are obviously a variation of the
refrain-like couplet of *The City in the Sea*; it is dark, grim
and despairing in the manner of that poem; it borrows
scenic effects from *The City in the Sea*, *Dream-Land* and
The Haunted Palace; and it uses a language constantly
reminiscent of these and other poems by Poe. It is distinct
chiefly because it describes a city of *industrial* death
(shades of Arnold again), because its language is more
restrained than Poe's and because here and there it seizes
on an image of fear which is free of derivativeness and
artificiality.

I have quoted *The City of the End of Things* below and
followed it with some notes illustrating its relation to Poe.
Since there is no space to quote more than the immediately relevant lines and passages from Poe, the reader who
wants to pursue the matter further should consult his
works.

THE CITY OF THE END OF THINGS

1. Beside the pounding cataracts
2. Of midnight streams unknown to us
3. 'Tis builded in the leafless tracts
4. And valleys huge of Tartarus.
5. Lurid and lofty and vast it seems;
6. It hath no rounded name that rings,
7. But I have heard it called in dreams
8. The City of the End of Things.
9. Its roofs and iron towers have grown
10. None knoweth how high within the night,
11. But in its murky streets far down
12. A flaming terrible and bright
13. Shakes all the shadows stalking there,
14. Across the walls, across the floors,
15. And shifts upon the upper air
16. From out a thousand furnace doors;
17. And all the while an awful sound
18. Keeps roaring on continually,
19. And crashes in the ceaseless round
20. Of a gigantic harmony.
21. Through its grim depths re-echoing
22. And all its weary height of walls,
23. With measured roar and iron ring,
24. The inhuman music lifts and falls.
25. Where no thing rests and no man is,
26. And only fire and night hold sway;
27. The beat, the thunder and the hiss
28. Cease not, and change not, night or day,
29. And moving at unheard commands,
30. The abysses and vast fires between,
31. Flit figures that with clanking hands
32. Obey a hideous routine;
33. They are not flesh, they are not bone,
34. They see not with the human eye,
35. And from their iron lips is blown
36. A dreadful and monotonous cry;

37. And whoso of our mortal race
38. Should find that city unaware,
39. Lean Death would smite him face to face,
40. And blanch him with its venomed air:
41. Or caught by the terrific spell,
42. Each thread of memory snapt and cut,
43. His soul would shrivel and its shell
44. Go rattling like an empty nut.
45. It was not always so, but once,
46. In days that no man thinks upon,
47. Fair voices echoed from its stones,
48. The light above it leaped and shone:
49. Once there were multitudes of men,
50. That built that city in their pride,
51. Until its might was made, and then
52. They withered age by age and died.
53. But now of that prodigious race,
54. Three only in an iron tower,
55. Set like carved idols face to face,
56. Remain the masters of its power;
57. And at the city gate a fourth,
58. Gigantic and with dreadful eyes,
59. Sits looking toward the lightless north,
60. Beyond the reach of memories;
61. Fast rooted to the lurid floor,
62. A bulk that never moves a jot,
63. In his pale body dwells no more,
64. Or mind or soul,—an idiot!
65. But sometime in the end those three
66. Shall perish and their hands be still,
67. And with the master's touch shall flee
68. Their incommunicable skill.
69. A stillness absolute as death
70. Along the slacking wheels shall lie,
71. And, flagging at a single breath,
72. The fires shall moulder out and die.

73. The roar shall vanish at its height,
74. And over that tremendous town
75. The silence of eternal night
76. Shall gather close and settle down.
77. All its grim grandeur, tower and hall,
78. Shall be abandoned utterly,
79. And into rust and dust shall fall
80. From century to century;
81. Nor ever living thing shall grow,
82. Nor trunk of tree, nor blade of grass;
83. No drop shall fall, no wind shall blow,
84. Nor sound of any foot shall pass:
85. Alone of its accursed state,
86. One thing the hand of Time shall spare,
87. For the grim Idiot at the gate
88. Is deathless and eternal there.

NOTES

1-2. "the pounding cataracts/Of midnight streams." **Cf.** "Bottomless streams and boundless floods . . . Seas that restlessly aspire" (*Dream-Land*).

2. "midnight." Cf. "the long nighttime of that town" (*The City in the Sea*) and "an Eidolon named Night" (*Dream-Land*).

2. "unknown to us." Cf. "a wild weird clime that lieth sublime/Out of SPACE—out of TIME" (*Dream-Land*) and "Resemble nothing that is ours" (*The City in the Sea*).

3. "tracts." Cf. Poe's use of "clime," "region" and "lands" in *Dream-Land*, and his use of "tract" in the first sentence of *The Fall of the House of Usher*, in which *The Haunted Palace* is quoted.

4. "valley." Poe makes great play with the word "valley" in *The Haunted Palace*: "The greenest of our valleys," "Wanderers in that happy valley," and "Travellers now within that valley."

4. "Tartarus." Cf. Poe's use of exotic-sounding proper names.

5. "Lurid" and "vast" are favorite Poe modifiers. Cf. "But light from out the lurid sea . . ." (*The City in the Sea*) and "Vast forms, that move fantastically . . ." (*The Haunted Palace*).
Poe is addicted to cumulative effects such as Lampman uses in this line. Cf. "Mute, motionless, aghast" (*To One in Paradise*) and "Their lone waters, lone and dead/Their sad waters, sad and chilly" (*Dream-Land*).

6. "rounded name." Cf. Poe's use of the word "name" in *The Raven*, *Silence*, *Dream-Land*, *Zanthe*, *Tamberlane* and *To Isadore*, and his obsession with certain names, especially the names of women—Ulalume, Lenore, Eulalie and Helen.

5. & 7. "seems-dreams" is perhaps the favorite Poe rime, only less popular with him than "dreams-beams," "dreams-gleams" and "dreams-streams."

8. Cf. Poe's title *The City in the Sea*. The word "thing," used very often by Poe in a supernatural sense, has a suggestion of the supernatural in Lampman's title. Cf. his use of the word in lines 25, 81 and 86.

9. "iron towers." Cf. "towers that tremble not" (*The City in the Sea*).

10-11. Cf. "Far down within the dim West" (*The City in the Sea*).

12-36 incl. Cf. "And travellers now, within that valley,

> Through the red-litten windows see
> Vast forms, that move fantastically
> To a discordant melody,
> While, like a ghastly rapid river,
> Through the pale door
> A hideous throng rush out forever
> And laugh—but smile no more.
>
> (*The Haunted Palace*)

Cf. especially "red-litten" here with Lampman's "flaming terrible and bright"; "vast forms" with his "stalking shadows" and "figures . . . with clanking hands"; "discordant melody" with his "awful sound" and "inhuman music"; and "A hideous throng" with his "figures that . . . obey a hideous routine." Note also line 27 in Lampman—"The beat, the thunder and the hiss"—another example of the composition by compilation so characteristic of Poe.

In writing this passage in *The City of the End of Things* Lampman may also have been influenced by Poe's *The Sleeper*:

> The bodiless airs, a wizard rout,
> Flit through thy chamber in and out,
> And wave the curtain canopy
> So fitfully—so carefully—
> Above the closed and fringed lid
> 'Neath which thy slumbering soul lies hid,
> That, o'er the wall and down the floor,
> Like ghosts the shadows rise and fall!

Lampman's lines 13-14, "Shakes all the stalking shadows there/Across the walls, across the floor," may be a reminiscence of the last two lines here.

37-39 incl. Cf.

> But the traveller, travelling through it,
> May not, dare not openly view it;
> Never its mysteries are exposed
> To the weak human eye unclosed;
> So wills its King who hath forbid
> The uplifting of the fringed lid."
>   (*Dream-Land*)

The King in Poe's passage is also death.

45-50 inc. Cf.

> Once a fair and stately palace—
>   Radiant palace—reared its head . . .

> Banners yellow, glorious, golden,
>   On its roof did float and flow,
> (This—all this—was in the olden
>   Time long ago,) . . .
>
> Wanderers in that happy valley,
>   Through two luminous windows, saw
> Spirits moving musically,
>   To a lute's well-tuned law . . .
>   (*The Haunted Palace*)

Cf. also,

> But light from out the lurid sea
> Streams up the turrets silently—
> Gleams up the pinnacles far and free—
> Up domes—up spires—up kingly halls—
> Up fanes—up Babylon-like walls—
> Up shadowy long-forgotten bowers
> Of sculptured ivy and stone flowers—
> Up many and many a marvellous shrine
> Where wreathèd friezes intertwine
> The viol, the violet and the vine.
>   (*The City in the Sea*)

These two poems, and *The City of the End of Things*, all involve a contrast between death or madness and a state of paradisal bliss. *The City of the End of Things*, and *The City in the Sea*, develop this contrast in an identical manner: they begin with images of death, then evoke memories of a blissful happiness, and end with a prophecy of utter destruction.

55. "idols." Cf. "In each idol's diamond eye" (*The City in the Sea*).

57-59. Cf.

> And from a proud tower in the town
> Death looks gigantically down.
>   (*The City in the Sea*)

58. "Gigantic." Poe is very fond of superlatives, and Lampman's poem abounds in this *type* of word: ceaseless, terrific, eternal, prodigious, continually, incommunicable, absolute, tremendous, utterly and deathless.

63. "no more." The phrase is Poe's trademark. It is stressed in several of his poems, and the "more" is usually rimed with "floor" or "door."

72. One would expect this line to read, "The fires shall *smoulder* out and die." The word "moulder" is distinctively Poe.

73-76 inc. Cf.

> And when, amid no earthly moans,
> Down, down that town shall settle hence . . . .
> *(The City in the Sea)*

82-83. Cf.

> For no ripples curl, alas!
> Along that wilderness of glass—
> No swellings tell that winds may be
> Upon some far-off happier sea—
> No heavings hint that winds have been
> On seas less hideously serene.
> *(The City in the Sea)*

85-88 inc. Cf.

> Hell, rising from a thousand thrones,
> Shall do it reverence.
> *(The City in the Sea)*

(The criticism of Canadian writing most often made by reviewers abroad may be summed up in one word: colonial. This opinion conflicts with that of many Canadian critics, who believe that Canadian writing, at its best, has always escaped from a derivative dependence on

*English and American writing and attained a level of
quality that entitles it to the serious interest of readers
anywhere. Who is more nearly right—the Canadian or the
foreign critic? The above analysis of Archibald Lampman
is the third in a series of articles, intended to offer an
answer to this question by examining the relation of the
Canadian writer to his literary influences. Other articles
will appear from time to time.—Ed).*

A READING OF LAMPMAN'S "HEAT"

DESMOND PACEY

All critics of Archibald Lampman, and notably Duncan
Campbell Scott, Carl Y. Connor, Raymond Knister,
Norman C. Guthrie and E. K. Brown, have agreed that he
was one of the most conscientious craftsmen in the history
of Canadian poetry. They have confined themselves, however, either to general appreciations of his skill, or to the
analysis of a few selected lines. So far as I am aware, no
one has undertaken the full dress analysis of a Lampman
poem as an organic whole, and that is the purpose of this
article. I propose to examine the famous "Heat," because
it is the poem which I know and like best and because it
is easily assessable. Since it is in almost every Canadian
anthology, I shall quote from it sparingly, assuming that
the interested reader will provide himself with the text.

Many readers must have felt that "Heat" has a fascination out of proportion to its surface meaning. It is, of
course, remarkable enough for its descriptive accuracy,
perfection of tone and unwavering concreteness. Here

"A Reading of Lampman's 'Heat,'" by Desmond Pacey. In *Culture* 14
(September 1953), 292-297. By permission of the author.

beyond doubt, is a typical Ontario summer day, caught as cleanly as words could ever catch it. The plains "reel" in the strong sunlight both in the sense that they unwind from the eye to the horizon like a fisherman's line and that they seem, in the currents of hot air, to waver back and forth like a drunken man. This latter effect of the atmosphere also explains the poet's choice of the word "swim" to describe the progress of the road as it nears the top of the hill. The poem throughout is filled with examples of such verbal exactitude: the wheels of the haycart, slightly loose on their axles, are said to be "clacking," which is the precise onomatopoeic word to describe that odd but familiar sound; the slow song of the thrush is exactly expressed in the description of him "sliding" his "thin revolving tune," as is the more shrill and rapid chirrup of the grasshopper by the contrasting "spin."

But this accuracy, this exact translation of sensation into word, does not of itself seem sufficient to explain the spell which the poem weaves. Nor is the secret, I think, in the metre and melody of the verse, apt and haunting as they are. Lampman has used stanzas of eight lines, rhyming ababeded, and of these lines the first seven are in iambic tetrameter and the eighth in iambic trimeter. This final shorter line has the opposite effect to that of Spenser's final alexandrine: instead of bringing each stanza to a majestic close and suggesting a pause, it implies inconclusiveness and urges us on to the next stanza. Lampman, in other words, is less interested here in painting a series of tableaux than in projecting a linked sequence of emotional impressions.

As in his choice of stanza form, Lampman has shown great tact in varying the metrical pattern to suit his special purposes. In the first stanza, for example, a trochee replaces the iamb in the first foot of each of the third and fifth lines for the obvious purpose of suggesting the difficulty of the upward climb of the road and the wagon. In the third stanza, the first foot of the second line is inverted to suggest that the extraordinary power of the sun as it "soaks in the grass," and the third line has an extrametrical syllable to provide the retarded pace necessary for the act of counting the marguerites one by one. Similar metrical modifications, all clearly justified, can be found in each of the stanzas.

Similar skill is evident in Lampman's use of alliteration and assonance. As we might expect in a poem whose subject is slow, silent, summer heat, the most heavily alliterated consonant is "s." In the first stanza we get "southward," "steep," "seems," "swim," "summit, slowly steals"; in the second, "side," "slouching slowly," "sky to sky," and "sole"; in the third, "the sun soaks," "still," "spider"; in the fifth, "spin," "small," "sound," "sometimes," "skyline," "sight"; and in the sixth stanza "sharp," "sweet," and "sloped shadow." For all this, the alliteration is seldom if ever overdone: the repeated sibilants and labials have their effect but they do not, with the possible exception of the line "Is slouching slowly at his ease," obtrude themselves.

Lampman's cunning and functional use of assonance can perhaps best be illustrated by examining the four middle lines of the second stanza:

> Half-hidden in the windless blur
> Of white dust puffing to his knees.
> This wagon on the height above,
> From sky to sky on either hand. . . .

The short "i" and short "u" vowels of the former two lines suggest the close-up effect of the picture: here the eyes, as also the vocal organs in pronouncing the vowels, are being held within narrow limits. In the latter two lines, as the scope of the picture broadens and our eyes are invited to view the scene panoramically, the long "i" vowels allow our mouths to expand also.

But not even yet, it seems to me, have we reached the essence of the poem's appeal. To do that, we must consider

the imagery, and see how cunningly Lampman has woven
and interwoven certain motifs.

The poem is constructed on the principle of balanced
opposites: dry is set over against wet, hot against cold,
light against dark, near against far. Let us look at each of
these pairs in turn.

The clay road being "white" is dry, but it seems to
"swim"; cart and wagoner are dusty, but the sun "soaks"
in the grass; the water-bugs are close to the water of the
brook, elm-tree shadows are like a "flood," but the burnt
grass is dry and the ground is "droughty."

Heat is suggested almost continuously throughout the
poem—by words such as "melt," "heat-held land," "burning," and "full furnace"—but cold is there too, in "the
cool gloom" beneath the bridge and in the shade of the
trees.

Now for the light-dark antithesis. The distant plains of
the opening line are "dim," but the road is "white and
bare"; the wagoner is half-hidden in dust but the wagon
is bright against the skyline; the marguerites are so clear
in the sunlight that they can be individually counted, but
the water-bugs are in the shadow of the bridge; the elm
trees cast shadows but the thrush is singing into "the pale
depth of the noon," the woods are "blue with haze" but
the hills are "drenched in light"; the poet is in "the sloped
shadow" of his hat, but he is also in "the full furnace" of
the hour.

The deliberate opposition of near and far is equally
apparent. The first stanza is panoramic until the last two
lines, when the eyes, having swept the horizon, come to
rest on the wheels of the haycart. The first half of the
second stanza continues the close-up effect; then the gaze
widens to take in the whole panorama again. In the third
stanza we begin with panorama and then narrow down
to the flowers and tiny insects near at hand. The fourth
stanza gradually leads the eye from the nearby trees and
cows to the limitless distance suggested by "the pale depth

of the noon," and much the same is true of the fifth stanza, where we are carried from the grasshoppers and crickets to the distant woods and hills. And in the final stanza the ultimate in narrowing is effected as we are brought completely away from the external world into the poet's mind.

There are several other types of physical contrast in the poem: the slow song of the thrush against the rapid chirp of the grasshopper, the tiny midges and water-bugs against the great hills and woods, for example. But the principle of balanced opposites does not merely apply here to physical things: it applies also on the personal and the cosmic planes. There are two persons in the poem, and they are as unlike as two men could well be. One is the wagoner, the manual labourer, the other the poet, the sensitive intellectual. And in the lines

> Beyond me in the fields the sun
> Soaks in the grass and hath his will

we have at least an implicit suggestion of the ancient cosmogony, widely diffused in myth and legend, whereby all creation is the result of the intercourse of the male Sun with the female Earth.

But if the poem merely set forth, and did not reconcile or unify, these sets of opposites, it would be interesting but not as significant as it really is. Readers of this poem are often puzzled by the final stanza; some critics have even gone so far as to consider it superfluous; I think it provides the essential clue to the poem's meaning. Lampman asserts that "In the full furnace of this hour" his thoughts have grown "clean and clear." He also says (in an obvious reference to the pairs of opposites of which we have seen the poem to be composed) that to him "not this or that/Is always sharp or always sweet." What he is claiming, and claiming justly as I hope to demonstrate in a moment, is that somehow this experience has brought him a special insight, a moment of vision, an epiphany. He has become aware of both the full sharpness and the full

sweetness of life, and of them both at once and as necessary
complements of each other. The same applies to all the
pairs of opposites in the poem; wetness and dryness, heat
and cold, light and dark, near and far, fast and slow, are
not merely opposites but complements of one another.
Similarly, the wagoner is the complement of the poet, and
the Sun of the Earth.

That it is Lampman's real theme to reveal and reconcile these opposites can be demonstrated from the way in
which he deliberately links them, and weaves them in the
pattern of a larger unity. The wagoner is linked with the
poet by the phrases used to describe them: the wagoner
"is slouching slowly at his ease," the poet "leans at rest."
The grasshopper is linked with the thrush in that the
song of each is said to revolve in the air. But it is this
notion of revolution, of cyclical movement, the dominant
image of the whole poem, which is the chief means by
which these seemingly incompatible opposites are reconciled.

We see this image most clearly in the "idly clacking
wheels" of the haycart, the "thin revolving tune" of the
thrush, and the spinning song of the grasshopper, but once
we have become aware of it we can see it almost everywhere. Cyclical movement is suggested by the "reel" of the
plains (whether it be the weaving circles of the drunkard
or the unwinding fisherman's reel that we envisage), by
the "puffing" of the dust around the wagoner's feet, by
the sun (its circular shape and its diurnal revolution), by
the marguerites with their spokelike petals, by the rumi-
nant cows with their slowly turning cuds. It is also suggested by the rhythm of the lines: throughout there is a
gentle rise and fall as of a slowly moving wheel. Look, for
example, at the first two lines: the voice rises to "reel,"
slowly sinks to "dim," rises again to "by," and falls to
"bare." Circular motion is also conveyed by the structure
of each stanza: in each the eye is invited to make the

circuit of the horizon and then to settle on a specific point of rest.

This dominant image of the turning wheel is symbolic of the unity of the poet's experience, and of the vision of a unified world which this moment of insight has vouchsafed to him. The turning wheel is Lampman's version of that glimpse of eternity which Vaughan described as a ring of pure and endless light. The wheel slowly turns, and as it turns light succeeds dark, heat cold, dry wet, and so on. These opposites are the spokes of the wheel: they have their place in an endless cycle which gives them each meaning and a final unity.

This may be, of course, to read too much into an apparently simple nature lyric, though I have sought throughout to follow the poem's own suggestions and to discover its pattern upon it. Whether the poet consciously put all these suggestions there seems to me irrelevant: any poet must work at least in part intuitively, and especially when he is seeking to project a mystical moment of vision.

I trust that I have at least demonstrated that there is a little more to Lampman's poetry than meets the casual eye. For my own part, I fully subscribe to the assertion of Norman Gregor Guthrie that Lampman's verse "looks at its best through the microscope." "His verse," Guthrie writes, "is of a texture and character that commends itself to the most intimate study and re-reading. . . ." If this article has provoked some careful re-reading, I shall be satisfied.

THE SIGNIFICANCE OF LAMPMAN

LOUIS DUDEK

Of the four leading poets of Canada writing in English before 1900, Archibald Lampman, who was the least appreciated in his lifetime, commands most respect, offers the most interesting perspective of ideas, and has most to say to the poets writing today. The other three, Bliss Carman, Charles G. D. Roberts, and Duncan Campbell Scott, may have other virtues and provide lessons of another kind; but Lampman in many ways comes closer to ideas and concerns still with us, problems that may even loom larger with time. He was in many ways looking ahead, with something of a pained squint, and the things he saw are worth considering more closely from our present more uncompromising point of view.[1]

The worst complaint we have to make of the others of that generation is that they have adopted a number of pat formulae, derived at third or fourth hand from English romanticism, and they repeat these again and again in superficial lyrics of no fresh perception or thought: Carman, for example, repeats his message of spontaneous joy to the point of nausea, and Roberts gives us doses of transcendentalism in soporific quantities. Lampman, too, has his share of these handy romantic formulae: "Nature"

"The Significance of Lampman," by Louis Dudek. In *Culture* 18 (September 1957), 277-90. By permission of Mr. Dudek, who has recently made minor revisions to improve the style.

[1] Too little has been written on Lampman. The studies of Norman G. Guthrie and of Carl Y. Connor, as well as E. K. Brown's critique, are in many ways defective and need to be supplemented by contemporary criticism that will look at the subject with more up-to-date ideas and criteria than those of pre-1930 Canada. A good biographical study is also needed; none at all now exists apart from D. C. Scott's memoir in the Collected Poems.

as the great refuge, the comforter; "the city" as a repository of "greed" and "strife"; the greenery of trees as a presage of autumn, of eventual death; the tiny bird as the teacher of Nature's great lesson, and so forth. But in Lampman some of these formulae assume the proportions of a private myth; Lampman's own early death (at the age of 37) turns the Keatsian death-lament[2] into genuine tragic premonition, and his rejection of the city is an expression of his real radicalism in politics and his discomfort as a petty civil servant in the jobbing and patronage-corrupted capital of Canada. Moreover, personal integrity in Lampman narrows down the pat romanticism of his themes to what is absolutely essential for his own poetry.

But more important than this apt use of the romantic tradition is the tone of sadness and deep pessimism that pervades all of Lampman's poetry. He is the only poet in Canada before 1900 who possesses the significant ground-tone of all valuable poetry elsewhere in that period. Before the onset of the modern movement, whether in the "terrible sonnets" of Hopkins, or the stoical life-despair of Housman, or the philosophical pessimism of Hardy or of Robinson, a dark melancholia reveals itself in the more important poets writing in English before 1910; facile optimism, following the Victorian urge to see the bright side of God, Nature, and Man, is found in the lesser poets, in Stevenson, in Lanier, in Carman and Roberts. Lampman differs from his Canadian contemporaries as the only poet in Canada who belongs in spirit to the company of Hardy, Robinson, Emily Dickinson and Housman, not of Alice Meynell and her friends.

The note of suffering, sometimes raised to the scale of cosmic sadness, is the very keynote of Lampman's poetry. At the personal level, he reveals the temperament of the

[2]For some direct and indirect references to death, see *The Poems of Archibald Lampman* (Toronto 1900), pp. 10, 19, 21, 23, 23-24, 27, 27-30, 62, 75, 84, 217, 243. This book is the posthumous collection of Lampman's work, referred to as his Collected Poems.

typical melancholic, undergoing alternate phases of depression and sudden relief. This provides a pattern of central experience for his poetry. As an expression of romantic imagination, his temperament reminds us of De Vigny or Leopardi; and nearest to Lampman, of course, his contemporary Thomas Hardy. But raised to a philosophical plane, it reveals a questioning and troubled view of nature and man, a dissatisfaction with the complacencies of the popular romantic formula and moves toward new positions of doubt and mental struggle.

A great deal is implicit, therefore, in the pessimism of Lampman. On the one hand, it is the most subtle expression of his social criticism; and on the other, it points to a searching philosophical bent of mind that makes him a forerunner of the significant poetry in this century, wrestling in ideational terms with problems of fundamental emotion and belief. Lampman thought of himself always as the poet; he speaks in the role of a conscious poet, according to Wordsworth's definition, opposed to the busy man of the crowded city. By means of this antithesis, and the specific life experience from which it gathers force, he reveals the difficulty of the poet's position in a rudimentary and practical culture, in "a business civilization," as E. K. Brown calls it. And in his inevitable and persistent note of sadness, almost of despair, in depicting nature, Lampman invites an investigation of the roots of this emotion, and thus leads us directly into the climate of poetry that follows his age.

We can see this best, perhaps, by considering the needs of poetry in Canada and how Lampman succeeded or failed in filling these needs. He is the only poet in the Group of '61 who looked sharply at the political and human facts of life. As a radical socialist, he viewed politics critically, if somewhat theoretically; and, as a minor civil servant in Ottawa, he could report at close range on the irritations of our political affairs. This is precisely what was needed, or part of what was needed, in a Canadian poet.

A new country is not a land for Lotos Eaters. Open to
every kind of future development, limited as yet in every
way, it needs observers, surveyors, critics—in short, gadflies.
A poet born on this "barren waste, unprofitable strand"[3]
needs energy, conviction, resistance and persistence, to
make his position clear and to define his function. He cannot be a mere servant of beauty; we are not a decadent
country but an emergent one. He must strive for a higher
order for a civilization; not a "business civilization," but
a larger scope of imaginative life in variety and freedom.

Lampman had many of the qualifications for this work
of a poet in Canada: he had a high sense of dedication, a
deep social awareness and an irritability that springs from
that fact, and a care for substance as the core of poetry—in
other words, a moral character that goes with the Miltonic
and Wordsworthian view of the poet. But he had two
obstacles standing in his way which prevented the full
realization of his talents and limited the development of
his poetry: his ill health, and his half-hearted commitment
to an outworn aesthetic.

Like the explorer and pioneer, the poet in Canada needs
a strong constitution to do the work required. Lampman
suffered a setback in health in his boyhood from which he
never recovered and which left him a prey to heart disease.
A severe attack of rheumatic fever at the age of seven kept
him bedridden six months and left him lame for the next
four years; the disease often leaves its mark and may
shorten the span of life itself. Lampman had been an active
athletic boy until that time, and even afterwards always
showed a penchant for the life of healthy activity outdoors;
but his personality after this illness seems to have been
touched by the shadow and he was "physically the least
powerful" in both school and college.[4] He resigned himself
after graduation to a quiet desk job in the Post Office

---

[3]From Standish O'Grady's *The Emigrant.*
[4]Duncan Campbell Scott, Memoir in Lampman's Collected Poems, p.
xv.

Department in Ottawa, despite his great promise at
Trinity College, and later refused even a library appointment in Boston when it was offered to him. One feels, in
reading the sketches of his life given by D. C. Scott that
here was a life of rich possibility hampered at the beginning by a tragic damage; and that the evidence of this will
appear inevitably in the poetry.

Among the Millet (1888), his first book, published at his
own expense, reveals a characteristic sadness of tone and
a preoccupation with death. This personal tone and theme
combine with his intellectual viewpoint to give his poetry
a great integrity of emotion and content, but at the same
time they strike at the root of the poet's energy for more
objective tasks and drain his spirit of an aggressiveness
which an active and varied life would have demanded.

Lampman's reflections on death and mortality take on a
virtually allegorical form in the numerous poems of
autumn and winter in his work. His most characteristic
comment on nature is an elegiac one, in which he foresees
the death of all things, with the coming of autumn, or of
winter. Nature even in spring and summer is only celebrated in order to introduce the elegiac note—that autumn
comes, and then the snows! In other words, Lampman's
subject is the universal one of death, and he uses nature
poetry to illustrate it on a large scale.

Thus, introducing the poem "In October" in an elegiac
mood, he intuits that "death is at the door, / So many low
soft masses for the dying / Sweet leaves that live not more."[5]
The entire poem must then be read, at one level, in the
light of that personal application. So too the other poems,
where "death grows vaster," where we taste of summer "ere
the quick death slay / The beautiful life that he hath in
chase"; and meet "The shining majesty of him that smites /
And slays you with a smile."[6] Autumn is Lampman's preferred season, because its theme is that of mortality, and

[5] Collected Poems, p. 21.
[6] Ibid., pp. 23, 27.

nature itself a kind of twilight realm where he tells us that
"Care and the battle of life shall cease."[7]

There is a more subtle and a very beautiful treatment of
the same subject in the poem "Winter Hues Recalled."[8]
Here he seems to refer directly to weakness of the heart
(as he does also in the poem "Freedom,"[9] where "our
tired hearts rest,/Loosen, and halt, and regather their
dreams. . . ."); a description of physical weariness and short
breath is achieved in halting Wordsworthian blank verse:

> Ere yet I turned
> With long stride homeward, being heated
> With the loose swinging motion, weary too,
> Not uninclined to rest, a buried fence,
> Whose topmost log just shouldered from the snow,
> Made me a seat. . . .

The poem presents a revelation of life in all its beauty,
seen in winter, while the poet in his entrancement "stood,/
Nor felt the keen wind and the deadly air" as he watched
the sun set before "the uprearing night/Remorsefully soft
and sweet." He closes with the significant lines:

> Then I awoke
> As from a dream, and from my shoulders shook
> The warning chill, till then unfelt, unfeared.

The central drama, a personal one, which gives the
motive to Lampman's poetry of melancholy, thus becomes
clear. The surface meaning of a poem like the one above
may be read, "It was cold, and time to go home"; the
organic unity of the whole poem, and the detail of epithet
and tone, turn upon the larger idea of life under the chill
shadow of death. In Lampman, since the feeling is often
precise but the exact intellectual motive is missing, the

[7]Ibid., p. 19.
[8]Ibid., pp. 27-30.
[9]Ibid., pp. 17-19.

carryover from one poem to another is often useful: the poem "The City" gives us explicitly a clue to the one of the readings of "The City of the End of Things"; and "The Poet's Song" suggests a possible reading of the poem "Heat," since the heat of day is there associated with the "half-mad" activity of the busy world from which the poet remains removed. In the same way, concern with death, and even an affection of the heart, may be traced from poem to poem "The Organist" ends with the death of the protagonist from heart-failure; and in "The Monk" we read how "Nino's heart had sprung/With sudden start as from a spectre's kiss." One need not make too much of these allusions, and they were probably deeper than Lampman's own awareness went; but they leap from the poems, and the autumnal tone of Lampman's poetry is unquestionably the Keatsian one of death, made entirely Lampman's own by his tragic and similar fate.[10]

But if this subject brings pathos and universality to his poetry, it also limits the scope of his imagination and the range of his perceptions. Preoccupation with one grand universal theme, touched off by fear of organic weakness and debility, induced a habit of caution into his life and his writing, and sapped his energy for the more daring struggle which he might have undertaken. In the poems, a state of "peace," of "rest," becomes his primary aim—a debilitating ideal that disposes of all real achievement in exchange for "dream," or at best the occasional imaginative vision of action:

Impetuous deeds that woke the God within us.

One recalls Gide's hero in *L'Immoraliste,* who blamed his dying wife for a similar weakness. Or Nietzsche on the false virtues of "peace and good sleep." Lampman too

---

[10]In his second book, *Lyrics of Earth* (1895), written mainly after his marriage, Lampman seems to adopt an optimistic, if superficial, tone for a time; but before long he returns to his normal and more convincing despondency.

often wishes to secede entirely from the world of action,
"Nor think but only dream";[11] and the one saving grace
is that his nature does not permit him this luxury. He
thinks, and thinks too much, for he was capable by nature
of a rich participation in active and intellectual life. As
most critics have perceived from the beginning, the criticism of Lampman turns naturally to the topic of possibilities unrealized."

Lampman's thinking, however, brings us to the second
part of his difficult development as a poet. This has to do
with his conception of poetry and the philosophical cast of
his ideas. On the one hand, he inherits from the nineteenth century a good part of the worshipful pantheistic
vision of nature; and he feels himself called upon to
embody this vision in a classical poetic form. In this
respect he shows himself an extremely conventional poet
walking in the footsteps of his masters. On the other hand,
some radical non-conforming scepticism within him fails
to live up to this poetic ideal and produces a sense of
defeat and of psychic depression that, uniting perfectly
with the poet's temperamental needs, results in a poetry of
great integrity and depth.

In contrast to his contemporaries, there is in Lampman's
works a marked dearth of reference to God. Not that
Lampman, an Anglican clergyman's son, would be an un-
believer or an atheist—he sometimes did take the theistic
short-cut to resolution—but that the fulcrum of his intellectual position lay elsewhere. God in his poetry appears,
for instance, under the scientific appellation "Energy." He
speaks of God as "The Energy, serene and pure," in two
poems, "Peccavi, Domine" and "The Clearer Self"; or
simply as "the energy divine" (uncapitalized) in a sonnet
titled "By the sea."[12] As a socialist, that is, a rationalist
in his approach to society, Lampman might be expected to
extend his critical thought to his religious ideas; and this

[11]Collected Poems, p. 14.
[12]Ibid., pp. 199, 219, 272.

is precisely what we find. In the poems dealing with religous themes there is a marked influence of nineteenth century scientific thought, the kind of thinking that bothers the poet much and arouses "perxplexity and pain," or "That aching dim discomfort of the brain," which makes him choose to escape to nature—"Nor think but only dream."[13] Thus, in the overloaded diction borrowed from Keats:

> Ah! I will set no more mine overtasked brain
>> To barren search and toil that beareth nought,
> For ever following with sore-footed pain
>> The crossing pathways of unbourned thought. . . .[14]

In his poem "Storm" the wind moans, "The same blind thought . . ./Seeking the same strange thing . . .", whatever it is that the human spirit seeks. And the poet hears a "piercing pensiveness" even the songs of birds, always the questing thought that he would rather escape for the quiet and serenity of dreaming nature.[15]

The nature of this perplexing thought that lies behind Lampman's poetry is never explicitly defined; he is certainly not a poet of ideas—that is his deficiency, that he failed to bring his mental strife into clear focus—but he appears in effect as an Arnoldian, concerned with the retreat of faith across the naked shingles of the world, and he is clearly influenced by rational science. A number of poems indicate a reading of ancient history and anthropology. The poem "An Ode to the Hills" shows him as an evolutionist—a point of view he reconciles with his special theism. A Protestant individualist, he proposes the ideal of a "priestless worship," communism, and the abolition of marriage, in the utopian poem "The Land of Pallas."[16] In a number of places he refers to the dissolution of faiths

---

[13]Ibid., pp. 6, 14, 16.
[14]Ibid., p. 14.
[15]Ibid., pp. 30-33, 135. "Pensive" is a favourite word with Lampman.
[16]Ibid., pp. 221, 201-210, On evolution, see also p. 199.

and the ephemeral nature of all beliefs. Thus the falling
leaves remind him of the "failing murmurs of some conquered creed"; in a sonnet he tells us how "faith shall
pass" and in another how all dogmatic religions are
marked for extinction in time.[17] Lampman's vision of
human destiny is depicted in "The City of the End of
Things," and in "Alcyone," in the latter of which a dead
planet prefigures the fate of our earth:

> a region where no faintest gust
> Of life comes ever, but the power of night
> Dwells stupendous and sublime,
> Limitless and void and lonely,
> A region mute with age, and peopled only
> With the dead and ruined dust
> Of worlds that lived eternities ago.[18]

And the sonnet entitled "To Chaucer" states more clearly
than any other the tenor of Lampman's religious reflections, as he contrasts our time with the fourteenth century:

> And God above was great and wise and good,
> Thy soul sufficient for its earthly span,
> Thy body brave and full of dancing blood.
> Such was thy faith, O master! We believe
> Neither in God, humanity, nor self;
> Even the votaries of place and pelf
> Pass by firm-footed, while we build and weave
> With doubt and restless care. Too well we see
> The drop of life lost in eternity.[19]

This kind of reflection, where, like Arnold, Lampman
mourns the passing of faith, seems to lie behind his philosophic despondency in contemplating nature. The Wordsworthian exaltation is not for him, while the mind presents
its burden of contemporary knowledge; so that Lampman,

---

[17]Ibid., pp. 22, 268, 285.
[18]Ibid., pp. 177-178.
[19]Ibid., p. 271.

at best, sees life as "Spectral and wonderful and strangely sad."[20] He has not the vigour, or the temerity, to pursue his ideas to an ultimate conclusion. The conflict between Wordsworth and Arnold remains unresolved; and hence, on the philosophic plane, he writes with that sadness and austerity which becomes his characteristic conclusion on the nature of life.

Lampman's poetry must be read, then, not as the unsatisfactory expression of a romantic vision, but as one of interesting tension between a desire to fulfil the romantic hope and an opposed view of man and nature which does not make such exaltation possible. The keynote of his poetry is complaint, or conflict, namely the resistance of his self-honesty to the pull of his idealism. His desire for an inspired vision of nature cannot be reconciled either with his new knowledge or his new belief. Yet he strives to remain true to the affirmative, positive, joyous view of the romantic poets; and is disappointed constantly by his inability to maintain that role.

Often, the form his poetic experience takes is that of a momentary illumination coming out of a state of melancholy—the crumb of satisfaction that his romantic spirit chances to receive. This experience is conveyed in the poem "In November," where the partial illumination appears as—

> A nameless and unnatural cheer,
> A pleasure secret and austere.[21]

The same sensation occurs in the well-known poem "Heat" and in a score of others. Lampman does not pursue his intuition, and refrains from attributing to it any religious significance or even attaching it to his general view of nature. There was, perhaps, the beginning of a fresh metaphysical idea in the insight—different from the great pantheistic vision—something like the idea suggested in the

[20]Ibid., p. 110.
[21]Ibid., pp. 158-160.

poem "The Clearer Self"; but Lampman is content to allow it to stand, as a first ray of light, an insight into the austere and sad reality of things as they are.

As the poem "Alcyone" confirms, Lampman's view of man's fate is a tragic one; he sees an incomprehensible search for meaning in "the clear abyss of mind" ending in ultimate extinction of life on our planet—a tragedy which, like the cold star, remains immensely poignant, and beautiful, and mysterious. This, in effect, provides the note of austerity to his poetry. Like Hardy, whom he resembles in this, Lampman does best when he comes to terms with his negative vision and gives it trenchant expression. For however much he tries to be the romantic seer, the truth forces through; the formula of nature as the great comforter, as entire harmony, and the duty of the poet to achieve joy, in order to justify himself, all these fade before the conviction he gives of his inner unrest, melancholy, and pervading pessimism.

Lampman is not at his best, therefore, as a purely descriptive nature poet (though Canadian critics were bound to think so); he is at his best—and this was his own opinion —as a writer of sonnets; especially those direct declarative sonnets, patterned on Milton and Wordsworth, expressing moral indignation, intellectual conflict, a noble struggle with the world. I would cite as examples the sonnets "Despondency," "The Poets," "The Truth," "Knowledge," "An Old Lesson from the Fields," "Voices of Earth," "To a Millionaire," "The Modern Politician," "To an Ultra-Protestant," "Avarice," as some of his best and most authentic work. That book *A Century of Sonnets* (a title from Keats) which he had hoped for but which he could never get published, would have shown us more of the essential Lampman than did *Among the Millet* or *Lyrics of Earth*, books overweighed with melancholy nature poetry and Victorian romantic narrative.

He wrote too much of the second kind, of course, too

much poetry in which he goes to nature as a refuge from life, in order to dream of life:

> Beyond the tumult of the mills,
> And all the city's sound and strife,
> Beyond the waste, beyond the hills,
> I look far out and dream of life.[22]

And too often his nature poetry presents a pastoral of nature, too perfect and peaceful to be true (I do not find the Laurentian black fly or the whining mosquito in his idylls); so that here, in his own element, a lack of realism is his undoing. True, there are fine detailed descriptions of the Ottawa countryside; but the total picture is wrong, askew from reality. It is a pastoral dream of innocence and of good, not the peasant's or the botanist's real world; and it is offered to us as a faithful picture of nature and of the true life—in other words, as part of that romantic dream which Lampman's own truth-seeking and austere mind contradicted. When he deals with the city, with commerce, and wealth, or even with his own inner doubts and anguish divorced from the nature idyll, he is a realist; he reports the fact as he really knows it, not as he would like it to be. But just then he fails to draw upon his imagination.

Finding his solace in nature and in "dreaming of life," Lampman consciously leaves behind him the city and the real life of men. His pose of high poetic vocation, so conspicuous throughout, becomes unconvincing, since it is all too clear that he is abandoning his post as imaginative interpreter of men in order to doze over a fictitious "nature" at peace with itself. Both his flight, however, and the view of nature which it involves, belong to that weaker side of the poet—his physical debility, and his outdated romanticism—which the stronger part militates against and sometimes conquers.

It follows from this that the poems dealing with the

---

[22]Ibid., p. 153.

city, with social questions, and with ideas, although not Lampman's preferred subjects, since he would rather eschew them, are his most significant work. They are certainly the most revealing object lesson for other poets, particularly for poets in Canada. And, as in the case of his groping with the concept of nature, Lampman's position is ambiguous here, and it is satisfactory only in so far as he does tackle this subject matter forthrightly and deals with it in a trenchant manner. Since he does this, to some extent, he takes his place as the first fundamental critic of our culture and our political life; but again his failure to carry these ideas to their full poetic expression is the defect of the poems.

Lampman summarizes the life of the city and the principle of our economic system by the word "strife," a word which he uses in numerous contexts, but always weighted with the same associations. The technical term in political science would be *competition*. Since he is repelled by the competitive acquisitive nature of modern life, he finds little to interest him in the life of his city Ottawa, or for that matter in Canada. The attitude is characteristic of our leading poets: the life is there, but its human quality has been so devitalized that they find nothing to arouse the imagination in the actual round of business activities and entertainments. James Reaney, recently living in Winnipeg, has remarked on the CBC that he finds "nothing at all to write about" in the flatlands of the midwest; our Toronto poets—with one notable exception, i.e., Raymond Souster—have shown an extraordinary lack of interest in their own environment. Lampman wrote in his time that the Canadian poet "must depend solely upon himself and nature". Our life seems barren and maybe in many ways it is; but maybe its very barrenness is subject for poetry (as Flaubert proved in the novel, Eliot in poetry), and we need to look much closer at people and at the idea we have of them (and of art) before we can go beyond the barrenness to discover an unknown country.

Lampman, for the most part, like most of our poets, turned away from the reality of people and wrote about a fiction known to the nineteenth century poets as "Nature."

The peculiarity of Lampman's position is that he turned away (with a curse) from the actuality of political and social reality, which he found repugnant, and assumed that he could find "the true life," as he called it, elsewhere, in the vegetable world of nature. Hence he wrote utopias: the pastoral poetry of nature, and "The Land of Pallas," in which a politicial utopia is described. As for the real politicial and social life of Canada, the best he could envision for it was total destruction, annihilation—as we see in the poems "Alcyone" and "City of the End of Things." In fact, Lampman predicted a civilization-destroying war as the culmination of the present worship of power and money.[23]

In his awareness of social evil, however, we wish now that Lampman had been more specific, that he had given us the detail of his gesture as well as the last judgment. But at least he generalizes his social comment into a powerful idea and gives vent to his social (or anti-social) passions with tremendous force in the political sonnets we have on record.[24] In all these sonnets, we find great vigour of direct statement combined with extreme generality and absence of occasion or of specific detail. It is as though the blueprint for a project of poetry had been conceived, but the building itself had never been erected.

Both in his nature philosophy and in his social criticism,

[23]Ibid., p. 244.
[24]In his lifetime, the poem "Freedom" was the only piece in the Millet book to shew something of his political radicalism, while no poem of this kind was included in the second book, *Lyrics of Earth*, published by Copeland and Day, Boston. The best sonnets were unpublished until the posthumous *Collected Poems* appeared; in fact a few had to wait for the book *At the Long Sault* in 1943. The iconoclasm of Lampman in private life was not revealed (it was in fact cautiously smoothed over) until recently, when it was shown clearly in a selection of his letters published by Arthur Bourinot. So that this side of Lampman's poetry has hardly been adequately represented or evaluated.

therefore, Lampman holds an ambivalent position in that he fails to carry through his potential ideas to their full conclusions. The cause of this incompleteness may be explained by temperament, or by the limitations imposed by poor health and restricted life. Whatever the reasons, Lampman failed in both the philosophical and political dimensions to develop his real energy to the fullest as a poet. His poetry remains one of unresolved tension and incomplete statement. Despite his clarity and precision of style, the lines "plated close and true,"[25] there is, owing to this ambivalence, sometimes an occult or veiled meaning implied in his best poems that he is unable to clarify: hence the apparently private meaning in poems like "Heat," "In November," "Midnight," and "Winter Hues Recalled."

In his philosophical poems, Lampman eschews a position of forthright and analytical pessimism, although that was the only way in his case to make any advance. In his social and political diatribes, he lacks the bold energy to go to the center of his subject and display grossness in detail and with particularity. How we would love to have a searching down-to-earth picture of Ottawa as Lampman saw it, done in prose, and the imaginative correlative of this in poetry! What we have is an essentially abstract poetry of unresolved inner conflict, of unease, and of inexplicable sadness. He is least satisfactory when he betrays this tension to sing the gay lyric celebrating nature. He is more satisfactory when he fails to repress and writes a poem of outright condemnation or, as in the sonnet "Despondency," of personal dejection. But neither of these direct forms of expression had been given a chance to ripen, nor were the intellectual structures prepared to support the emotions of reality and experience.

But as a poet of inward conflict Lampman offers an invaluable object lesson for the poets in Canada who follow

---

[25]Collected Poems, p. 5.

him. He shows where more daring is needed, more persistence, and more will to carry the battle to the world itself, not to an imaginary dreamland or utopia. The melancholy compromise, surely, is not for our times. We can now understand Lampman in a way that he could hardly understand himself. We have broken through the dilemmas that held him in suspense. We know too that laughter—a virtue he hardly ever displays in his poetry—can melt the fat off many an unresolved conflict and reveal the reality underlying illusion. We may try to do what he, if he had lived to see this century, would have approved, if he himself could not have shared it. In many ways, he remains a permanent guide and example. In the coming decades, there is every sign that we will suffer more and more from the pressures of politics and of institutional bureaucracy; we will also suffer from the life of pettiness and routine more than Lampman ever knew. "The City of the End of Things" is fast becoming a reality. Against that, Lampman's truthful self-scrutiny, and conviction, and refusal to submit, can be a weapon in behalf of the human individual.

THE MASKS OF ARCHIBALD LAMPMAN

F. W. WATT

> *They who shall see me in that hour will ask*
> *What spirit or what fire could ever have been*
> *Within that yellow and discoloured mask. . . .*
> ("Death," July 1891)

Archibald Lampman went to Ottawa in 1883 to take up a minor clerical position in the Post Office Department, and he remained at that post except for brief vacations until a short time before his death in 1899, at the age of thirty-eight. During these sixteen years he wrote the handful of mild and sensitive nature poems upon which largely depends his claim to be the best of nineteenth-century Canadian poets; and he led a life which was externally as contemplative and uneventful as the poems imply. In a memoir his close friend D. C. Scott remarked on how fortunate the poet was to receive, during most of his creative life, the security of that undemanding Civil Service post, and to live in the small though growing city of Ottawa, which still permitted easy access to the rural scenes he so much loved. Yet from the evidence of letters and relatively unfamiliar parts of his prose and poetry, Lampman's life in Canada's capital city was not at all one of quiet fruitfulness, but on the contrary one of unrest, dissatisfaction often to the point of despair, and unresolved tension and conflict within himself and with the society in which he lived.

In the two years following his grateful acceptance of the Civil Service position (it relieved him of a brief and highly incompatible first career, that of school teacher), Lampman

---

From "The Masks of Archibald Lampman," by F. W. Watt. In *University of Toronto Quarterly* 27 (January 1958), 169-84. By permission of the author and the publisher, University of Toronto Press.

was complaining in letters to a friend[1] of a debilitating mood from which he could not escape and which was the opposite of contentment or happiness. He also referred in the letters to a curious species of writing he was attempting at this juncture:

I am in the midst now of the barren period; I cannot work; I have been writing at a voluminous fairy tale—and have composed many sheets of very monotonous rubbish. —I can do nothing but saw wood. (Dec. 10, 1884)

I have been very dull and out of spirits.—oppressed with innumerable things—debts; ill-success in everything, incapacity to write and want of any hopes of ever succeeding in it if I do. I cannot do anything—I believe I am the feeblest and most good-for nothing mortal any where living. . . . I wrote another fairy tale the other day—much to mother's disgust; who is unlimited in her complaints of the impractical and outlandish character of my writings, which indeed fetch no money—or even respect. As to the story I made it in a dull lifeless state of mind, so I dare say it is bad enough. . . . (Jan. 20, 1885)

In the first number of *Man* (Nov., 1885), the short-lived Ottawa periodical edited by Lampman's father-in-law, Dr. Edward Playter, there appeared what may well be a product of the kind of effort referred to in these letters, under the title "Hans Fingerhut's Frog Lesson." It has since been forgotten; but it contains what can be considered, though in the form of a fairy-tale, a symptom of Lampman's essential artistic and spiritual dilemma at a revealing moment, and as such it may prove worthy of examination even at some length.

In 1880, while still at Trinity College, Lampman had already shown a more than academic interest in the plight of certain exceptional men for whom, according to literary tradition, an unsympathetic society proved a cause of dangerous disillusionment. "What a delicate thing to

---

[1] Letters to Mrs. J. M. McKeggie, Trinity College Library.

be entrusted to this stern world's keeping is a poet's nature . . .", he said in an essay on Shelley.[2] "How easily it may be spoiled, embittered, and turned away from truth in an unaided struggle with the unsympathetic coldness and heartless oppression of society. . . ." Shelley's was such a nature, and Lampman described him as one who for this reason became a "pure worshipper of nature"; "his mind turned in weariness from the contemplation of what he had already seen of the deep-rooted evils of the world's society to a groping search (in nature) after truth." "Hans Fingerhut's Frog Lesson" tells of an experience in several respects not unlike this, but significantly only a hint or two is given in it of the existence of "evils of the world's society." In Lampman's story, as we shall see, the poet Hans Fingerhut is made to take upon his own shoulders all the responsibility for his alienation from the community.

The mythological pattern of the tale is familiar—that of a hero's separation or withdrawal from the world, his initiation into mysteries, and his return to society. "Long ago," it begins, "almost out of recollection, there lived in a small town in a woody German valley a poet named Hans Fingerhut." Hans, like Lampman himself, experienced a disappointing lack of success in his vocation. As a consequence the German's poems "began to grow peevish and querulous, and men would no longer listen to them as they had done to the fresh and joyous ones of his youth." This response only made him angrier, and now he "shrieked and thundered with songs full of wrath and bitterness," bringing ruin upon himself, for "the great people turned him from their gates." He then was obliged to set himself up as a tailor in order to support himself. "All day he sewed and stitched, and scowled at the passers by, and half the night he wandered about the streets, scrawling satires on the gates of all whom the people

[2]*Rouge et Noir*, I, no. 4 (December, 1880).

honoured." What relation this picture had to Lampman himself, chained to the drudgery of the Post Office clerkship of which he so often complained, is not difficult to see, and easier still with the details that follow:

Often as he sat and sewed, great songs seemed to come to him, beautiful visions and thoughts that dawned on him and sought to combine with the restless melody in his soul; but the remembrance of his disappointments and forlorn condition always turned them into chants so dreadful and ferocious that little children were afraid to pass his door.

Not unexpectedly Hans turned to the countryside for comfort, but he was so much at odds with his world that even the beauty of nature seemed to mock him. In a rage he tried to silence the music of a stream by which he had paused, and thereby he offended its guardian elf. A gesture from the elf, and Hans was transformed into that raucous and discordant creature, the frog, until he could learn to interpret correctly the "song of the stream" he had tried to destroy. The frog's life, he discovered, is miserable, precarious, and painful. Even his fellow frogs, with whom he joined in stridently objecting to their lot, were alienated from him:

The other frogs would have nothing to do with him; nay, even sat sometimes and abused him. For there was something uncanny about Hans Fingerhut. He talked often to himself in a tongue unknown to them. Sometimes he wept in silence—a thing which astonished them very much, for no other frogs could weep. . . .

At last, after all Hans's interpretations of the song proved to be wrong, the elf relented in pity, and Hans's own tears became fairies that sang the song to him in a language he could understand. The story's somewhat anti-climatic turning point, the "Song of the Water Drops," is an expression of cosmic optimism based on a stoical acceptance of one's lot and faith in Nature's maternal purposes. Once free, Hans took this new faith back with him to the town, where his life was transformed by it:

He no longer walked with his usual defiant stride, downcast face and scowling brow. The portly figures and round faces of the busy burghers, and the well-filled purses at their girdles no longer made him fierce and envious, but he greeted them all with a quiet and pleasant "good morning". . . . But from that day the great songs that he made were nothing like his former ones. There was never anything bitter or complaining in them. They were all sweet and beautiful and wise.

The tale of Hans Fingerhut concludes with a consummation not achieved in Lampman's own life; and there is, as we shall see, stronger proof of this than the very relevant description D. C. Scott gives in his memoir of Lampman's normal physical bearing: "In the city, he walked habitually with a downcast glance, with his eyes fixed upon the ground; in the fields and woods he was alert and observant." But undoubtedly Lampman's continual resort to the natural world was in its own way, as he said of Shelley, "a groping search after truth." Hope of success led him to that intense concentration of detail and mood in his nature poems which is their best quality; but the obvious failure in that search makes their limitation. On the other hand, he was not always ready to assume the whole burden of his recurring sense of alienation from his society. Unlike Hans, Lampman often felt the need for regeneration not only of himself, but of the social order as well, and when he did so it was not easy to settle the conflict within himself and with his society by a simple fairy-tale resolution.

Lampman's response to the world or even to the world of nature was always more varied and complex than the modest, sensitive, meticulous craftsmanship of his few best nature poems, such as "Heat," "In November," "A Sunset at Les Eboulements," would alone suggest. It is true, as these poems show, that he continually turned to rural scenes as the simplest kind of anodyne or release, but at other times he gave nature a more important role: she is shown in some poems as holding the key to moral laws which man, fallen from harmony with her, has lost and can find again only in communion with her. The belated Romanticism of this view must be called wilful rather than ignorant, for Lampman's "Man and Nature" asserts this faith in language which deliberately opposes the attack made by Matthew Arnold on the Romantic philosophy of nature—"Nature and man can never be fast friends. . . ." Lampman wrote:

> That only which is nature's friend shall find
>   Beauty's firm law and follow it aright;
> But long ago the children of mankind
>   Abandoned nature and sought other light,
> Made their own Gods, endowed with other power
>   And beauty left them at the self-same hour.

Whatever the theological status of "beauty," Lampman has here joined in the challenge of the Romantic and the radical to institutional religion. In a letter to E. W. Thomson on November 2, 1897, Lampman expressed his revulsion against institutional religion more bluntly, while admitting that his contacts with it were purposely rare, "about three times a year":

It always depresses me to go to church. In those prayers and terrible hymns of our service we are in the presence of all the suffering in the world since the beginning of time. . . . Sunday is a day that drives me almost to madness. The prim black and collars, the artificial dress of the women, the slow trouping to church, the bells, the silence, the dreariness, the occasional knots of sallow and unhealthy zealots whom one may meet at street corners whining over some awful point in theology,—all that gradually presses

me down till by Sunday night I am in despair and would
fain issue forth with pot and brush and colour the town
crimson.[3]

Despite the mild bravado of the last phrase, it was the
countryside around Ottawa rather than the wilder diver-
sions of the city itself that typically offered Lampman a
release from the excessive pieties of Victorian Canada. And
the poet sometimes believed that by communion with the
natural world he could escape not only these, but also all
the more sordid aspects of the modern industrial and commercial civilization.

"Freedom" states this more general attitude with a revealing explicitness:

> Out of the heart of the city . . .,
> Out of the heat of the usurer's hold,
>   From the horrible crash of the strong man's feet;
> Out of the shadow where pity is dying;
>   Out of the clamour where beauty is lying,
> Dead in the depth of the struggle for gold;
>   Out of the din and the glare of the street;
> Into the arms of our mother, we come,
>   Our broad strong mother, the innocent earth,
> Mother of all things beautiful, blameless. . . .

"Innocent" and "blameless" and their like were favourite
adjectives with Lampman. Against the dull, ugly, evil life
of men, especially men caught in the condition of expand-
ing industrial urbanism, Lampman opposed the archetypal
sanctuary of innocence he still saw in nature beyond the
borders of the cities. In "Favourites of Pan," the best
record of this prelapsarian creed, the frogs can speak with
the notes of the god Pan to those who wander "far from
the noise of cities and the strife"; and those who listen are
carried back to the first idyllic scene:

---

[3]*Archibald Lampman's Letters to Edward William Thomson (1890-
1898)*; ed. Arthur S. Bourinot (1956).

   . . . they that hear them are renewed
     By knowledge in some god-like touch conveyed,
  Entering again into the eternal mood
    Wherein the world was made.

More than a few of Lampman's contemporaries, impelled
no doubt by some of the same forces, sought through
nature to enter the peaceful land of Eden. Wilfred Campbell, for example, in his poem "In the River Bay," looks
for a refuge from "The new desire and old regret, / The
doubt, the sorrow, and the curse, / The passions that our
spirits nurse. . . ." He wishes,

       Refined, removed of all earth's dross,
       Its strife, its sorrow, and its loss,
       To be a little child for aye,
       Mist-cradled in this river-fay.
          (*Lake Lyrics*, 1889, 33-4)

That other pleasant country, paradoxically not far distant
from Eden for some writers—Bohemia—attracted relatively
few Canadians; and the Bohemianism of Carman and
Roberts was certainly no serious threat to respectability.
But Lampman was too restrained and too fastidious to
relax his moral tensions even with, for example, the innoc-
uous gusto of such a poem as Carman's "Isabel," in which
the note of burlesque is prominent but apparently quite
unconscious:

       In her body's perfect sweet
       Suppleness and languor meet—
       Arms that move like lapsing billows
       Breasts that Love would make his pillows,
       Eyes where vision melts in bliss,
       Lips that ripen to a kiss.
          (*Songs from Vagabondia,* 1894, 29)

Finding his consolations in the natural world, Lampman preferred to speak of easing the coils of human relations in a more decorous and oblique fashion. Thus his un-objectionable apostrophe "To a Flower" gives thanks that "I may come at any hour / And take thy beauty without fear":

> Thou hast no human smile to bless,
>   And not with tears thine eyes are wet;
> But I may love thee and caress,
>   Without reproach, without regret.

Lampman differed in another way from those late nine-teenth-century Canadian poets who at times slipped away from society into the delectable kingdoms of Eden or Bohemia: for him such an escape created a far greater degree of tension. He often felt a longing not to escape or withdraw but to enter more fully the everyday world of modern urban civilization. "I envy you to a certain extent your active life," he wrote to his college friend, the Reverend C. H. Shortt, "and I yearn for something of this kind in a dim way, as one of those Kentucky cave creatures, with their degenerated eyes might yearn for the faculty of sight." And he sometimes expressed regret at his lack of knowledge of politics and his inability to take a direct political role.[4] Far from being "somewhat indifferent to the social and economic currents about him," as E. K. Brown has suggested,[5] Lampman appears to have been interested to the point of fascination in the industrial urban conditions of his environment and all they entailed. His poetry shows him not merely rejecting them—though he obviously did this at times, as the traditional view of him suggests—but also coping with and trying to under-stand them. The latter response can be seen plainly in such poems as "A Night of Storm," which ends after its description of the city during a storm in an apostrophe that shifts

---

[4]Letters to the Reverend C. H. Shortt, Trinity College Library.
[5]*At the Long Sault* (1943), xvi.

the focus from the violence of nature to the violence
of human suffering:

> City of storm, in whose grey heart are hidden
>   What stormier woes, what lives that groan and beat,
> Stern and thin-cheeked, again time's heavier sleet,
>   Rude fates, hard hearts, and prisoning poverty.

"The Railway Station" shows in a similar way that the
poet was reaching out in sympathy to the lives of the city
dwellers he only dimly glimpsed. The poem describes a
train as it pulls out of the station:

So many souls within its dim recesses,
    So many bright, so many mournful eyes:
Mine eyes that watch grow fixed with dreams and guesses;
    What threads of life, what hidden histories,
What sweet or passionate dreams and dark distresses,
    What unknown thoughts, what various agonies!

More interesting than these is the poem called "The
City," in which Lampman exhibits, one could argue, a
work of peculiarly twentieth-century sensibility struggling
for birth in the womb of a nineteenth-century poetic
technique:

> I see the crowds for ever
>   Go by with hurrying feet;
> Through doors that darken never
>   I hear the engines beat.
>
> Through days and nights that follow
>   The hidden mill-wheel strains;
> In the midnight's windy hollow
>   I hear the roar of trains.
>
> Ah! the crowds that for ever are flowing—
>   They neither laugh nor weep—
> I see them coming and going,
>   Like things that move in sleep.

"A crowd flowed over London Bridge, so many," is perhaps only a step or two away in intentions, but Lampman's is an "Unreal City" in the wrong sense. If the attempt was to convey an impression of what was to him ugly, incongrous, but fascinating in the urban sense, the effect is inappropriately one of archaism and uneasy elevation—as in these lines from the same poem which presumably refer to the city's discordant night-life: "And the guest-hall boometh and shrilleth, / With the dance's mocking sound." Lampman possessed none of the techniques of naturalism, realism, or irony and he was both prepared and encouraged to write in a quite different mode. For this reason his most successful poem on the urban theme is cast in the lurid, melodramatic vein of James Thomson's "City of Dreadful Night." In Lampman's "The City of the End of Things" the perceptual phenomena of the modern city are presented not at all naturalistically, but are transformed into a symbolic vision or nightmare:

> . . . in its murky streets far down
> A flaming terrible and bright
> Shakes all the stalking shadows there,
> Across the walls, across the floors,
> And shifts upon the upper air
> From out a thousand furnace doors;
> And all the while an awful sound
> Keeps roaring on continually. . . .

The decay of spirit and humanity which takes place in the "city of the end of things" remains somewhat mysterious. But the relevance to Lampman's own problems as a poet is acute if we see in the "grim Idiot at the gate," sole survivor of the cursed city, "deathless and eternal there," Lampman's figuring of the creative spirit of the artist in the sterile condition to which the nightmare of rampant industrial urbanism might one day reduce it. The city portrayed in this way, in "its grim grandeur," is a potent symbol, but the effect is gained by the sacrifice of a good deal of the complexity of Lampman's feeling towards urbanism. It has the power and the weakness of a gross oversimplification. Whereas the countryside was at times simply Eden, the city has here become the antithetical kingdom of Hell.

There remain two other reactions of Lampman to industrial urban civilization to be considered; the first of these points to the poet's ideological position, and is to be found in the extensive utopian vision, "The Land of Pallas." The Land of Pallas is a familiar ideal, an egalitarian, communistic, peaceful, unchanging land of brotherly love, a "nowhere" more like Morris's than Butler's, though with characteristics of both. In Lampman's Utopia "all the earth was common," as Henry George in the Eighties and Nineties was insisting it should be, and there is community of ownership: "all the store of all to each man was his own." Both city and countryside are places of beauty. But it is evident from the poet's description that the reason lies partly in the agrarian nature of the economy; for his idlyllic society bases its livelihood not on industry but on the land. Lampman's Adamite inclination is obvious, too, in the poet's depiction of the State: it is anarchistic, relying for social order on the gospel rather than on the law:

> . . . there was no prison, power of arms, nor place,
> Where prince or judge held sway, for none was needed
> there . . . .

> And there were no bonds of contract, deed or marriage,
> No oath, nor any form, to make the word more sure,
> For no man dreamed of hurt, dishonour, or
> miscarriage. . . .

Returning after his stay in this land the narrator attempted to preach to his fellows the lessons it taught him, but understandably he "preached but fruitlessly; the powerful

from their stations / Rebuked (him) as an anarch, envious
and bad. . . ." Lampman wrote two endings for the poem,
one more pessimistic and harsh than the other:

> Then I returned upon my footsteps madly guessing,
>   And many a day thereafter with feet sad and sore
> I sought to win me back into that land of blessing,
>   But I had lost my way, nor could I find it more.

The narrator's initiation was evidently more disturbing
and more demanding than Hans Fingerhut's. The published version of the poem, though not altogether empha-
tically or clearly, avoids such despair by endorsing the
"idea of progress":

> And still I preached, and wrought, and still I bore my
>   message,
>   For well I knew that on and upward without cease
> The spirit works for ever, and by Faith and Presage
>   That somehow yet the end of human life is Peace.

The contrast between the Land of Pallas and the world
in which he led his daily life—even when the latter was
seen by the faint glow of attenuated optimism—was a sharp
and bitter one for Lampman. Coming out of the Land of
Pallas the narrator tells us he saw

> A land of baser men, whose coming and whose going
>   Were urged by fear, and hunger, and the curse of greed.

> I saw the proud and fortunate go by me, faring
>   In fatness and fine robes, the poor oppressing and slow,
> The faces of bowed men, and piteous women bearing
>   The burden of perpetual sorrow and the stamp of woe.

In another class of poems Lampman provided harsh
critiques of this land, contemporary society at its worst,
which are as remote from the utopian idealizations of

"The Land of Pallas" as they are from the negative
utopianism, so to speak, of "The City of the End of
Things." In poems like "The Modern Politician," "Liberty," "To a Millionaire," "Epitaph on a Rich Man," and
"The Usurer," criticism of what he takes to be features of
his own society is more directly applied. "What manner of
soul is his," he exclaimed in his attack on the "modern
politician," "to whom high truth / Is but the plaything of
a feverish hour, / A dangling ladder to the ghost of power!"
His is the "age of brass," the time of the "rich man" who

> . . . made himself a great name in his day,
> A glittering fellow on the world's hard way,
> He tilled and seeded and reaped plentifully
> From the black soil of human misery;—
> He won great riches, and they buried him
> With splendour that the people's want makes grim;
> But some day he shall not be called to mind
> Save as the curse and pestilence of his kind.

Lampman's detestation of the new plutocracy of industrial
civilization is apparent also in the conclusion of the sonnet
"To a Millionaire," where he holds the object of attack
responsible for

> . . . the unnumbered broken hearts
> The hunger and the mortal strife for bread,
> Old age and youth alike mistaught, misfed,
> By wants and rags and homelessness made vile,
> The griefs and hates, and all the meaner parts
> That balance thy one grim misgotten pile.

It is understandable that Archibald Lampman, with his
utopian visions of a finer social order and his critical sense
of the shortcomings of his own society, should have felt
himself estranged from many of his fellow Canadians,
especially in the Eighties and Nineties when national

ideals tended to predominate over all others. Lampman
was unwilling to seek popularity among the more enthu-
siastic Canadian nationalists. "At this time," he observed
quietly in a public lecture in 1891, "when our country's
destiny, its very independent existence perhaps, is a matter
of doubt and anxiety, it behoves us to be silent and do no
boasting, but look seriously about us for the wisest thing
to be said and done at each crisis."[6] He was incapable of
the patriotic fervour which inspired a writer like Charles
G. D. Roberts. "In the midst of our present political conditions," Lampman wrote a year later in his *Globe* causerie, "Mr. Roberts in his patriotic vein is a voice crying
in the wilderness, and he seems to have set himself in a
premeditated pose to cry there with all his might. . . . It
seems to me, however, that the times can hardly carry
patriotic verse, particularly of a boastful character. Satire
would appear to be the species of verse most applicable to
the present emergency."[7]

Although Lampman himself to a considerable degree
had the disposition and felt the desire to conform, the
pressures brought to bear upon him by his milieu to sub-
due his more bitter and more radical responses were still
greater. It was a rare critic who could interpret Lampman's
heretical poems in a way which suggested positive virtues
without denying their essential motivation. W. D. Light-
hall was one of these. In his journal *Horizon* (no. 1, 1903),
which was as shortlived as its motto would have led one
to expect—"A journal without Pretensions, Prejudices, or
Promises"—he praised Lampman for refusing to "bow the
knee to mammon" and asserted boldly, "Lampman keenly
felt the need of a new national ideal in our country, and
half consciously pictures the Canada-to-be in "The Land
of Pallas." The typical critical attitude to Lampman's

[6]Edited by E. K. Brown, in the *University of Toronto Quarterly*, XIII
(July, 1944), 407.
[7]"At the Mermaid Inn" (Nov. 19, 1892).

poetry in his own day was one of encouragment for its
mildness and its decorous restraint. "There is an absence
of the erotic," wrote Seranus in *The Week*, "of the merely
sensuous and vivid, of passion and colour and warmth for
their own sakes—the sin of the modern school—for which
the reader is thankful." And later, "A more startling, more
strictly original note might not leave so pleasant an impression, so potent a sense of calm powers undisturbed by all
the rude shocks of fate." (VI, 1888, 59.) To a passionate
and deeply disturbed poet this attitude was calculated to
be depressing. Equally dampening to certain aspects of
Lampman's inspiration, particularly his radical ardour,
must have been the eulogy of his poetry in *The Week's*
series, "Prominent Canadians," to which honoured élite
Lampman was raised in 1891:

Assuredly there is at times in some of the poems an unmistakable undertone of wistful regret for the prisoned fate of
the liberty-loving spirit but this is by no means akin to the
senseless ravings of shallower minds against the unpropitious environment of circumstances; and is far from vexing
the general serenity of the poet's even temperament. He
accepts life as he finds it, and leaves the madness of attempting to remake the world to fools who have no better task
in hand. (VIII, 1891, 299)

The commentary tells us more about its author and the
author's milieu than it does about Lampman, but it helps
to illuminate the kinds of tension which Lampman endured
while trying to discover and express "reality" as he experienced it. The easiest course was not to write poems which
would prove disturbing, or at least not to publish them.
This he did, by choice or necessity, in the case of a number
of his poems. A good example is "The True Life," written
in 1894, three years after he became a "prominent
Canadian" and one year before his election to the Royal

Society, but published for the first time in *At the Long Sault* in 1943:

> This life is a depressing compromise
> Between the soul and what it wills to do
> And what your careful neighbours plan for you,
> Often the thing most odious in your eyes,
> A makeshift truce. . . .
> O, world of little men, how sweet a thing
> The true life is, what strength and joy it hath,
> What grandeur and what beauty it might bring,
> Could we but sweep forever from our path
> your cant rules and your casuistries,
> Your clap-trap, and your damned hypocrisies.

An alternative to which Lampman resorted on another occasion effectively illustrates his problem. The *Globe* causerie of June 4, 1892, contains the poems "Falling Asleep" and "Reality," the latter (not elsewhere printed until recently) being in a bitter, sardonic mood the opposite of current ideas of the "poetical" and of the morally respectable. Lampman, it appears, sought to avoid a direct affronting of opinion by framing the poems in a short dramatic scene in which he attributes them to a mysterious friend who comes to visit him. "(My friend the sonneteer) knows in what abhorrence I hold those persons—so exasperatingly numerous in our time—who profane and misapply the sonnet, and he takes a sort of inhuman delight in torturing me with sonnets of his own composition on all sorts of flippant and improper subjects." The first sonnet is an introspective examination of the process indicated in its title, "Falling Asleep." After hearing it, Lampman says, he had the following conversation:

"Well," I said, "that doesn't seem to be so bad—in a certain sense, from a certain point of view—rather true to life, quite picturesque in fact—but could you not have arranged to cast your impression in some more suitable form a little less ridiculously inapplicable to the smallness and homeliness of your subject?" "No I couldn't," answered my friend, fixing me with a defiant glare. "The best way to impress your subject on the reader is to cast it in a totally unsuitable form. It's the contrast that does it, you know," and he took up the other paper, and read the following utterly atrocious and impudent production:—

REALITY

I stand at noon upon the heated flags
At the bleached crossing of two streets, and dream,
With brain scarce conscious, how the hurrying stream
Of noonday passengers is done. Two hags
Stand at an open doorway piled with bags
And jabber hideously. Just at their feet
A small, half-naked child screams in the street.
A blind man yonder, a mere hunch of rags,
Keeps the scant shadow of the eaves, and scowls,
Counting his coppers. Through the open glare
Thunders an empty waggon, from whose trail
A lean dog shoots into the startled square,
Wildly revolves and soothes its hapless tail,
Piercing the noon with intermittent howls.

"Certainly you have outdone yourself this time," I cried. "You have violated every law of moral dignity and literary decency" . . . The poor fellow has talent if he would only apply it in a serious and sensible way.

It is obvious that Lampman was not so scandalized by his friend the sonneteer, his alter ego, his Satanic spirit, or whoever he was, as a literal reading of the scene would suggest; he perhaps regretted that decorum would not allow longer and more fruitful visits. At any rate he allowed the second sonnet to stand in his manuscript book without any special apologies. The poet of "Reality," given the opportunity, might possibly have shown the way to a new poetic technique or to the mask that could have released Lampman's creative energies from the inhibitions of self and society by which they were plainly hampered. The figure of Hans Fingerhut, it will be evident by now, was just the opposite kind of mask. Hans was evidently a creation of Lampman's deepest despair and self-condemnation and his desire for peace of mind, and could not be more to him than what he once called

> A makeshift truce, whereby the soul denies
> The birthright of a being bright and new
> Puts on a mask and crushes down the true,
> And lolls behind a fence of courteous lies.
>   ("The True Life")

In such a mood Lampman accepted a view of poet and society which significant parts of his work belie. In the fairy-tale world of Hans, the poet displayed, not radical antagonisms to social evils, but simply envy of people more favoured; Hans's need was to find a way of conforming to that world as it was, not to try to remake it or to go beyond it. This was, in fact, the mask which Lampman's own mildness and the attitude of the intellectual milieu for which he wrote encouraged him to wear, all the more because his turning away from contemporary society and his quest for some arcanal, saving knowledge in the natural world produced a group of excellent nature poems.

Lampman's reactions neither to nature nor to the growing industrial urban civilization of his day could be contained within the persona of Hans Fingerhut, but he found no more adequate alternative. "In the wider politics," D. C. Scott said of him, "he was on the side of socialism and reasonable propaganda to that end, and announced his belief and argued it with courage whenever necessary."[8] His interest in radical ideas, however, found little encouragement in the predominantly conservative milieu of the Eighties and Nineties, and so he was able to do little more

---

[8]Preface to the Memorial Edition of Lampman's poems (1900).

than begin to explore naively this avenue of approach to
the subject-matter of city life which attracted him. The
tools or weapons of radicalism, along with those of naturalism (which offended the moral idealism of his society),
were largely denied him, and his intellectual capacities
and his social insights were that much weaker. Ultimately,
although he seems never to have abandoned the costly
effort to understand and give poetic form to his experience
in the contemporary world, Lampman was tempted—when
the opiate of the natural world failed him as it often did—
to place his faith in the kind of apocalyptic dream that
would reconcile radical idealism with conservative necessity. "If, all at once," he wrote in the *Globe* in 1892,
"through some strange moral awakening, men could be
got to see the miserable emptiness and vulgarity of the
desire for riches, the work of the social and political re-
former would be made beautifully straight before him,
and all things would adjust themselves to the ideal
plan. . . ." (Sept. 24) To this high and distant hope both
the poet of nature and the utopian socialist could return
from time to time to rest in an uneasy compromise.

It is impossible to know how aware Lampman himself
was of the self-contradictions and vacillations which, it
appears, he continued to endure throughout his sixteen
years in Ottawa; but there is no doubt that what he saw
as a lack of rigorous intellectual challenge and free play
of thought in his milieu consciously troubled him. "The
human mind is like a plant," he remarked in the *Globe*
causerie of August 27, 1892, "it blossoms in order to be
fertilized, and to bear seed it must come into actual contact with the mental dispersion of others." The Canadian
writer, however, "must depend solely upon himself and
nature. He is so much in the fructification of ideas."
Lampman seemed to recognize that his experience in
Canada was not unique, but the lot of most writers living
in a society where dialectic was discouraged, and in a ter-
rain where nature's simplicities and society's growing

complexities stood in vivid juxtaposition. Today Canadian writers have long since turned to new forms of thought and poetic expression, but they can still be found impaled on the horns of the familiar dilemma with which the earlier poet struggled. Lampman was not speaking for himself alone when he epitomized that dilemma with such neatness and sadness in this four line poem left forgotten in his manuscript book of 1892:

> Earth, heaven, and the mighty whole—
> I scan them and forget the strife;
> 'Tis when I read the human soul
> A darkness passes upon life.[9]

---

[9]Lampman MSS, Poems, 1889-92, University of Toronto Library.

BIBLIOGRAPHY

PRINCIPAL WORKS BY ARCHIBALD LAMPMAN

Among the Millet, and Other Poems. Ottawa: Durie, 1888, 151 pp.
Lampman's first collection of poems, privately published.

Lyrics of Earth. Boston: Copeland & Day, 1895, 56 pp.

Alcyone. Ottawa: Ogilvy, 1899. 110 pp.

Lampman had commissioned the private publication of this
book through T. and A. Constable of Edinburgh. He died
before the book could be issued, and Duncan Campbell Scott
instructed Constable to print twelve copies of the work for
limited distribution. *Alcyone* became part of *The Poems of
Archibald Lampman* (1900).

The Poems of Archibald Lampman. Edited with a Memoir by
Duncan Campbell Scott. Toronto: Morang, 1900, 473 pp.

This Memorial Edition has been the definitive collection of
Lampman's poetry. Duncan Campbell Scott's text and Memoir
have served as standard sources in Lampman scholarship. The
order and arrangement of the poems correspond to Lampman's
intentions insofar as these are apparent in the original editions
in which the poems first appeared, although there is some
evidence that Scott took editorial liberties with certain of the
poems.

Lyrics of Earth. Sonnets and Ballads. With an Introduction by
Duncan Campbell Scott. Toronto: Musson, 1925, 276 pp.

The title of this collection is misleading in view of the 1895
Lyrics of Earth. Poems in this volume are drawn from the
"collected" edition, although the arrangement is new. Particularly confusing is the first section of the book which is labelled
"Lyrics of Earth" but which is composed of poems which had
appeared in *Among the Millet* and *Lyrics of Earth.*

At the Long Sault and Other New Poems. Foreword by Duncan
Campbell Scott, Introduction by E. K. Brown. Toronto: Ryerson,
1943, 45 pp.

This is a selection of poems culled and edited for publication
from Lampman's notebooks by E. K. Brown.

Selected Poems of Archibald Lampman. Chosen, and with a Memoir by Duncan Campbell Scott. Toronto: Ryerson, 1947, 176 pp.

FURTHER MATERIAL ON ARCHIBALD LAMPMAN (SELECTED)

There are two book-length studies of Lampman, Norman Guthrie's modest *The Poetry of Archibald Lampman* (1927), and Carl Connor's *Archibald Lampman, Canadian Poet of Nature* (1929), both useful although somewhat dated. In addition the reader is referred to some of Lampman's letters which have been rather freely edited by Arthur S. Bourinot. Notably: *Archibald Lampman's Letters to Edward William Thomson, 1890-1898* (1956); *Some Letters of Duncan Campbell Scott, Archibald Lampman, and Others* (1959); also, *The Letters of Edward William Thomson to Archibald Lampman, 1891-1897* (1957) for the other half of the correspondence; and related material in *At the Mermaid Inn, Conducted by A. Lampman, W. W. Campbell, Duncan C. Scott* (1958).

Other valuable sources on Lampman not included in this collection for reasons of length or ready accessibility elsewhere are: Duncan Campbell Scott's "Memoir" which appeared in the Memorial Edition of Lampman's *Poems* (1900) and in modified form in subsequent collections of Lampman's poetry edited by Scott; E. K. Brown's chapter on Lampman in his *On Canadian Poetry* (rev. ed. 1944), and his Introduction to *At the Long Sault . . .* (1943); Munro Beattie's "Archibald Lampman" in *Our Living Tradition,* First Series (1957); Desmond Pacey's "Archibald Lampman" in his *Ten Canadian Poets* (1958); and Roy Daniells in his chapter dealing with Lampman in the *Literary History of Canada* (1966).